# A Teava Lady
# Who's Designed by God

## Reveals His Expressions
## Through Love Poetry

Written by Tea Lady D. Pearce

Cover and Interior Design by D. Pearce

D. Pearce
Legacy Tea House Society Club
6233 N 6th street
Philadelphia, Pa 19126

Ordering Information:
For details, contact ladiesoflegacysocietyteaclub@gmail.com

ISBN 979-8-9928801-6-8 (Hardback)
ISBN 979-8-9928801-5-1 (Paperback)

LCCN 2020917856

# Tea Table of Chapters

Tea Lady's Poetry of Love

# Wisdom

She is more precious than rubies;
nothing you desire can compare
with her.

**Proverbs 3:15 NIV**

I.

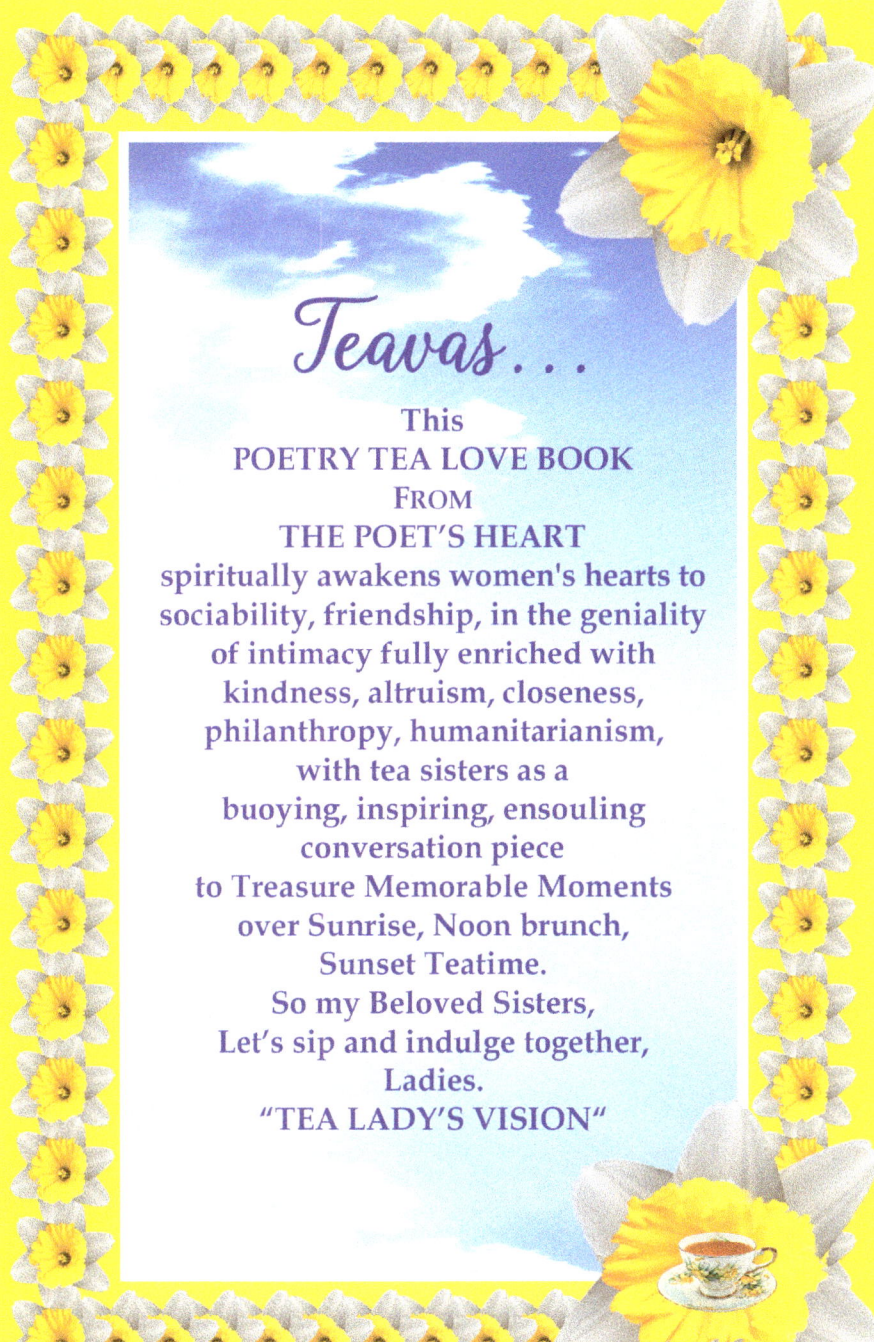

*Teavas...*

This
POETRY TEA LOVE BOOK
FROM
THE POET'S HEART
spiritually awakens women's hearts to
sociability, friendship, in the geniality
of intimacy fully enriched with
kindness, altruism, closeness,
philanthropy, humanitarianism,
with tea sisters as a
buoying, inspiring, ensouling
conversation piece
to Treasure Memorable Moments
over Sunrise, Noon brunch,
Sunset Teatime.
So my Beloved Sisters,
Let's sip and indulge together,
Ladies.
"TEA LADY'S VISION"

II.

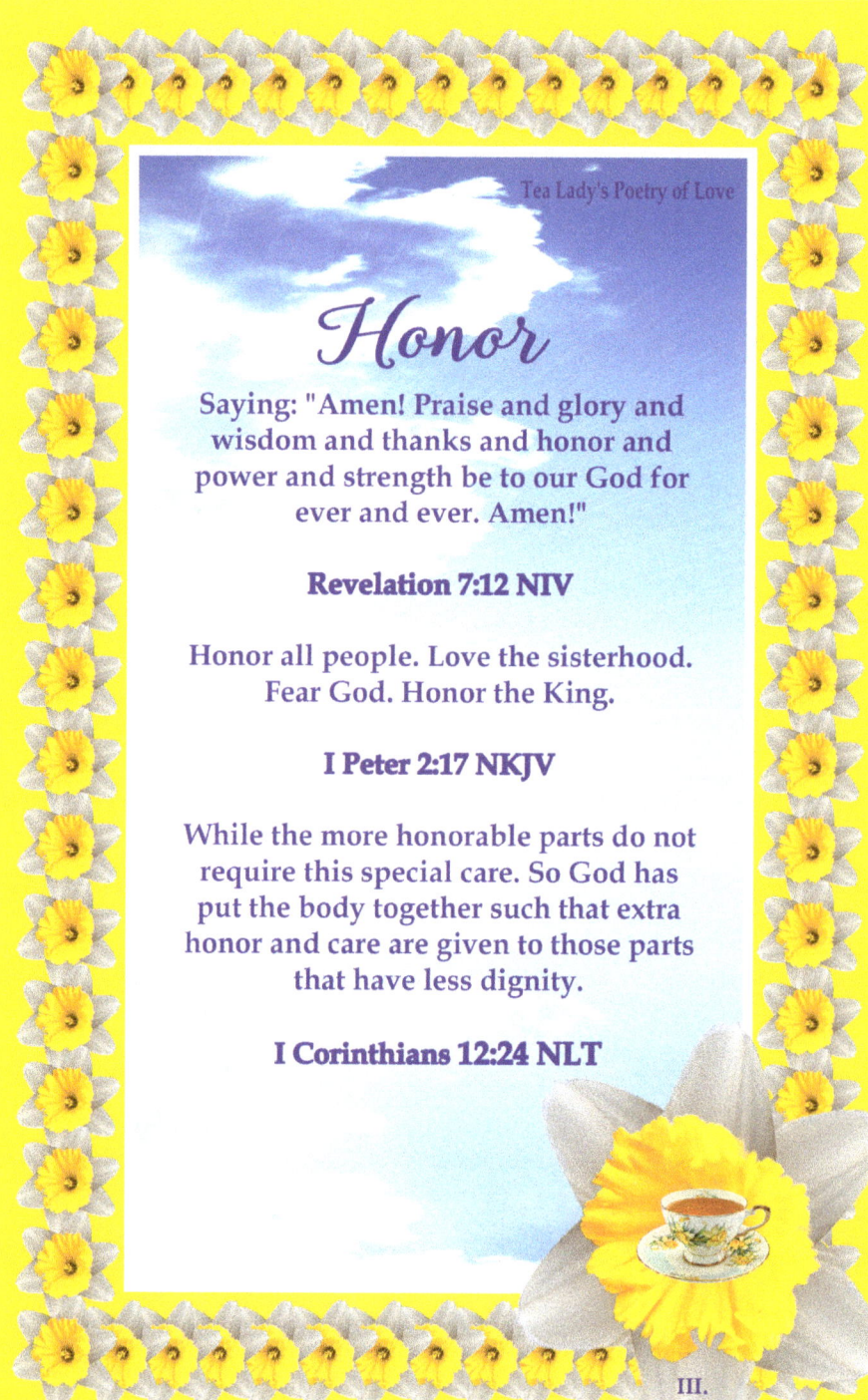

# Honor

Saying: "Amen! Praise and glory and wisdom and thanks and honor and power and strength be to our God for ever and ever. Amen!"

**Revelation 7:12 NIV**

Honor all people. Love the sisterhood. Fear God. Honor the King.

**I Peter 2:17 NKJV**

While the more honorable parts do not require this special care. So God has put the body together such that extra honor and care are given to those parts that have less dignity.

**I Corinthians 12:24 NLT**

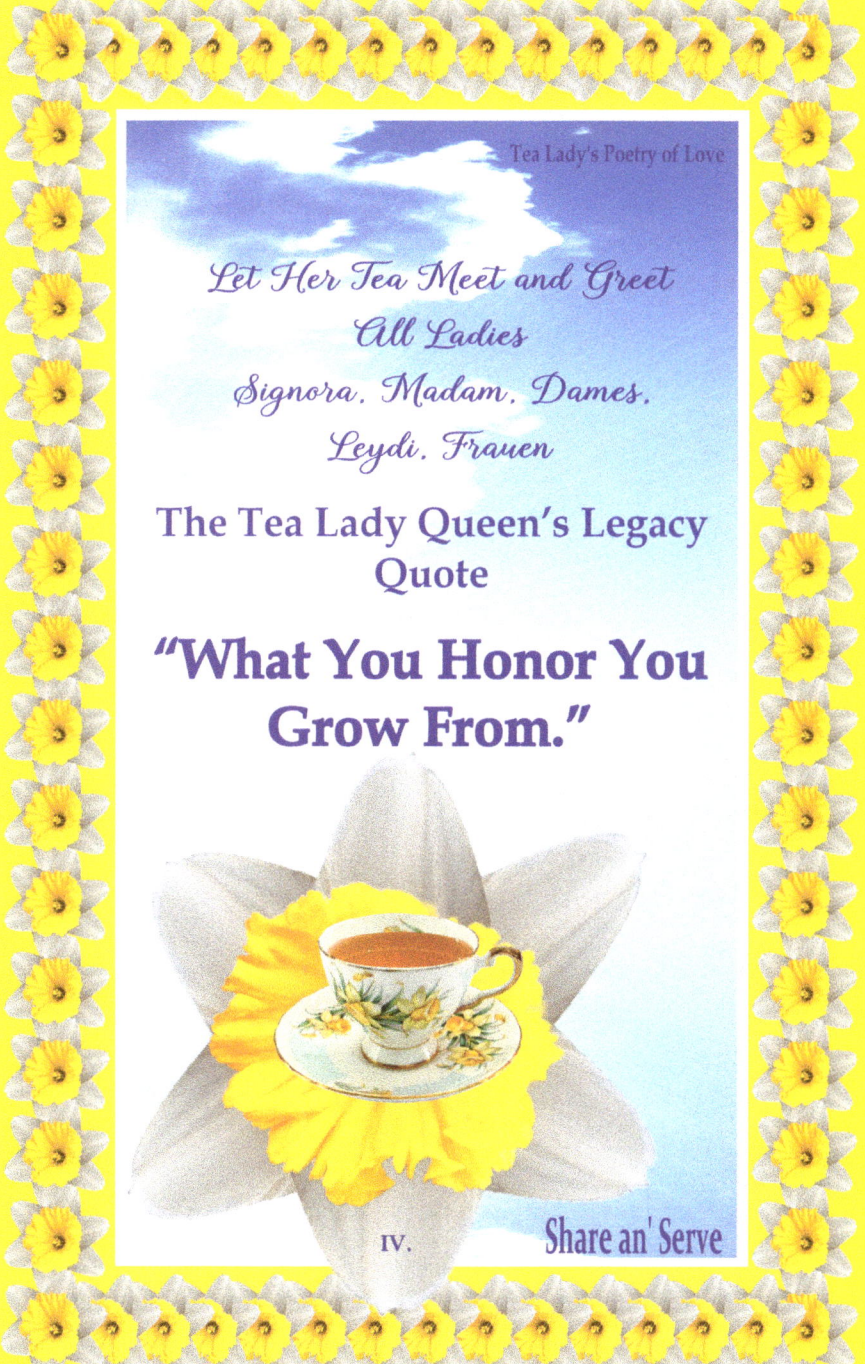

Tea Lady's Poetry of Love

*Let Her Tea Meet and Greet*
*All Ladies*
*Signora, Madam, Dames,*
*Leydi, Frauen*

## The Tea Lady Queen's Legacy Quote

# "What You Honor You Grow From."

IV.

Share an' Serve

# *Serving*
# *Tea Etiquette*

As each has received a gift, use it to
serve one another, as good stewards
of God's varied grace.

**1 Peter 4:10 ESV**

Sitting down, Jesus called the
Twelve and said, "Anyone who
wants to be first must be the very
last, and the servant of all."

**Mark 9:35 NIV**

v.

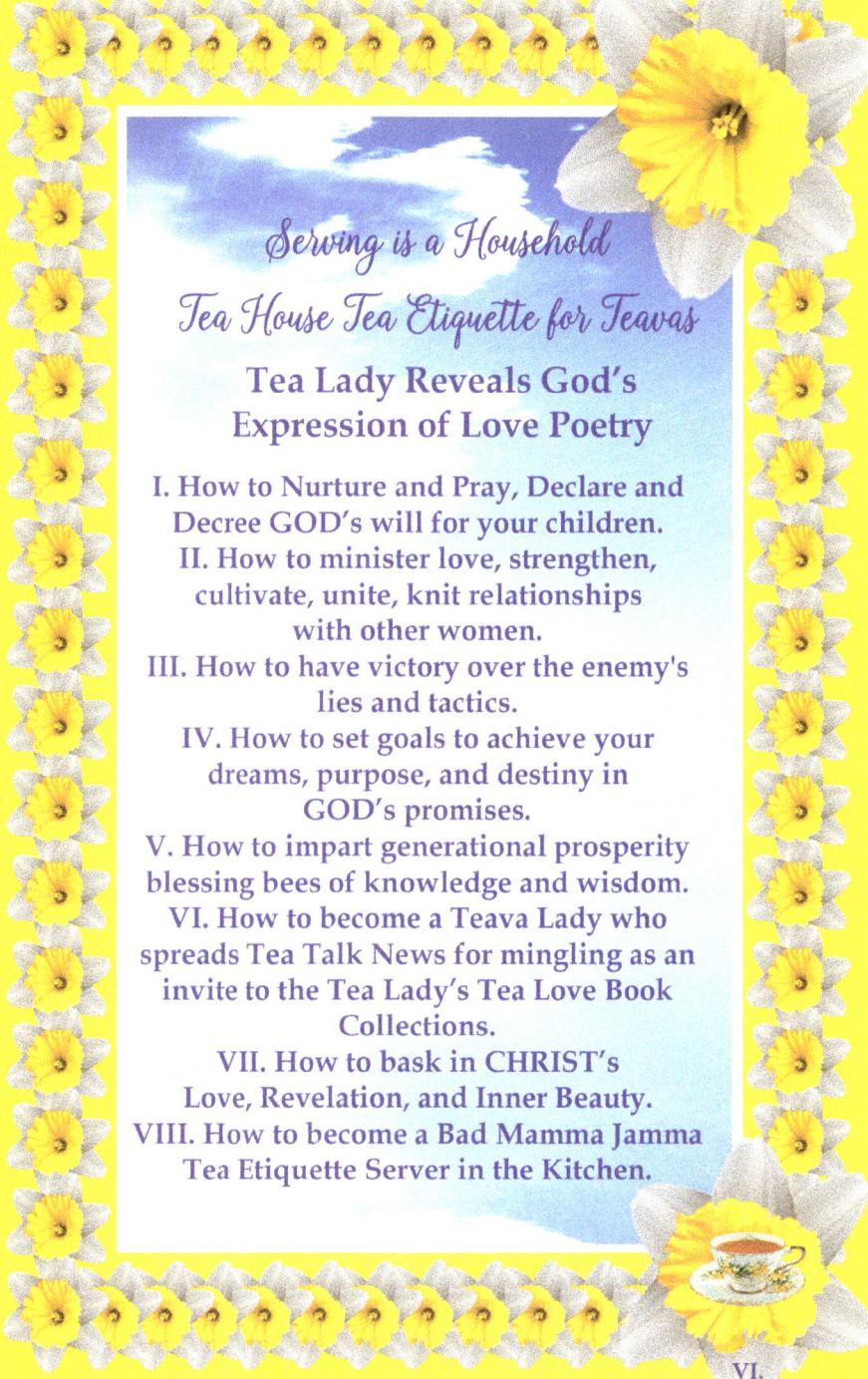

*Serving is a Household*

*Tea House Tea Etiquette for Teavas*

## Tea Lady Reveals God's Expression of Love Poetry

I. How to Nurture and Pray, Declare and Decree GOD's will for your children.
II. How to minister love, strengthen, cultivate, unite, knit relationships with other women.
III. How to have victory over the enemy's lies and tactics.
IV. How to set goals to achieve your dreams, purpose, and destiny in GOD's promises.
V. How to impart generational prosperity blessing bees of knowledge and wisdom.
VI. How to become a Teava Lady who spreads Tea Talk News for mingling as an invite to the Tea Lady's Tea Love Book Collections.
VII. How to bask in CHRIST's Love, Revelation, and Inner Beauty.
VIII. How to become a Bad Mamma Jamma Tea Etiquette Server in the Kitchen.

VI.

# Position

For if you remain silent at this
time, relief and deliverance for the
Jews will arise from another place,
but you and your father's family
will perish. And who knows but
that you have come to your royal
position for such a time as this?

**Esther 4:14 NIV**

## God Reveals...

A Teava Lady Who's Designed
In GOD's
divine will have been set and sent
in place from eternity,
for you to pamper in his
contentment as your "passionner."
Forwardly to share this Treasurable
Memoir Revelation.
Now let's come together,
my innocent buttercup,
honey sister-friend in
a comradeship formed in
light-hearted pleasurement over
teatime with
TEA LADY'S
HERBAL DELIGHTS CONVERSATION
TEA BLENDS TEAS
grown from her Tea Garden
Vineyards
where Wisdom is
Served.

# Thine

Thine eyes shall see the king in his beauty: they shall behold the land that is very far off.

**Isaiah 33:17 KJV**

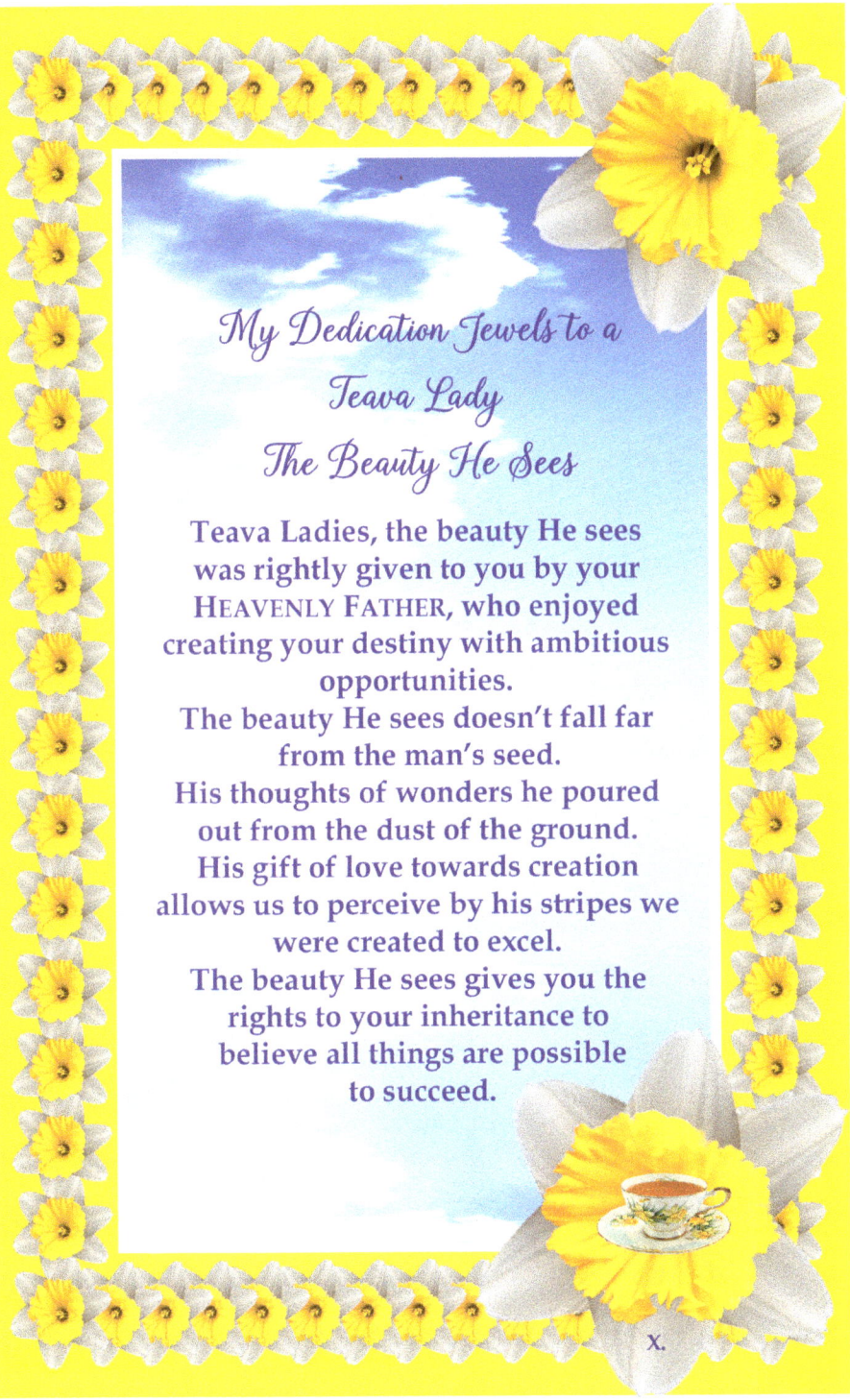

## My Dedication Jewels to a
## Teava Lady
## The Beauty He Sees

Teava Ladies, the beauty He sees
was rightly given to you by your
HEAVENLY FATHER, who enjoyed
creating your destiny with ambitious
opportunities.
The beauty He sees doesn't fall far
from the man's seed.
His thoughts of wonders he poured
out from the dust of the ground.
His gift of love towards creation
allows us to perceive by his stripes we
were created to excel.
The beauty He sees gives you the
rights to your inheritance to
believe all things are possible
to succeed.

X.

# Wise

**Every wise woman buildeth her house to stand.**

**Proverbs 14:1 KJV**

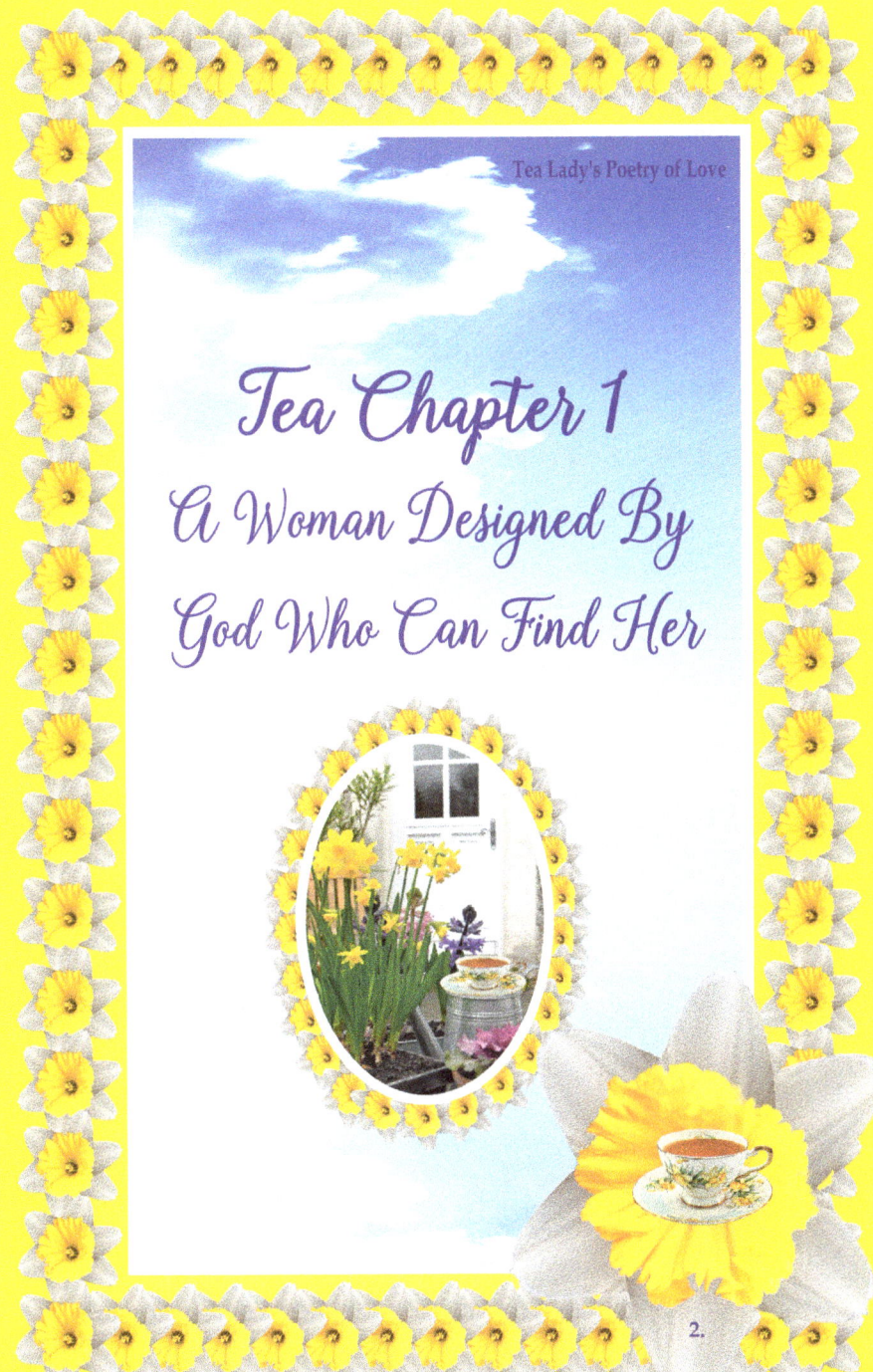

# Tea Chapter 1
## A Woman Designed By God Who Can Find Her

# *Find*

Who can find a virtuous woman,
for her price is far above rubies?
She openeth her mouth with wisdom,
and in her tongue is the law of
kindness. She looketh well to the
ways of her household, and eateth not
the bread of idleness.
Her children arise up, and call her
blessed; her husband also, and he
praiseth her. Many daughters have
done virtuously, but thou excellest
them all. Favour is deceitful, and
beauty is vain: but a woman that
feareth the Lord, she shall be praised.

**Proverbs 31:10, 26-30 KJV**

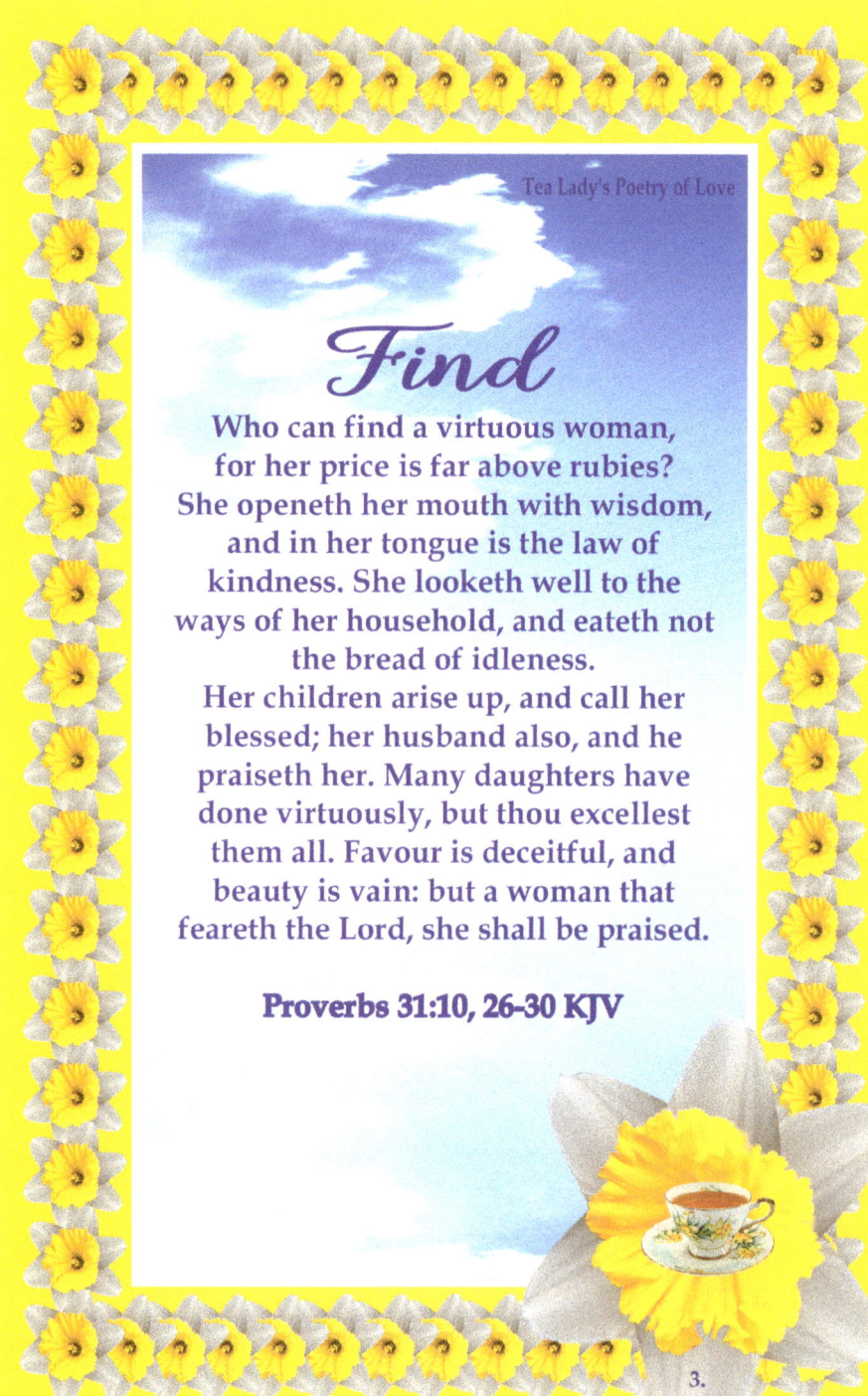

# A Virtuous Woman

A Virtuous Woman, so tender and meek,
She keeps her family upheld before the
LORD;
this is her sweet treat.
A Virtuous Woman
She's known for her accomplished repertoire
character that speaks volumes overflowing
in an abundance of discernment that gives
unconditional love because of her
Tea Language speech.
A Virtuous Woman
She puts her faith in
YESHUA, the DELIVERER, and SAVIOUR
THE KING OF THE JEWS
who is her stimulator, revelator, motivator,
and courier as He connects her with His
people whom she shall reach...
A Virtuous Woman
Her virtuous love knows her; no one can
compete because she stands in awe of her
KING.
She's a Woman of Virtue
who has been given the Keys to the
Kingdom of JEHOVAH-JIREH to release
faith, fervor, and favor to her descendants.
She's a Virtuous Woman who's a
TEA KEEPER, SOFTHEARTED,
TEATIME RELISHER.

Tea Lady's Poetry of Love

# Christ

I can do all things through Christ
who strengthens me.

**Philippians 4:13 NKJV**

5.

# Yes I Can

Yes, I can fly like a Tea Lady Eagle
that's ready to blossom.

Yes, God made me with so many
possibilities, eventualities, and
probabilities to pour out my tea kettle that
fully blooms.

Yes, I can reach my full potential as my
assigned ANGELIC HOSTS guide me athwart,
around Tea Shops and Tea Worlds, while my
aspirations, abilities, and goals will be safe,
rewarding, and secure with sound
endurance.

Yes, I can soar, as a Teava Lady Servant,
ready to serve; that's what I was put here for,
to take my sister-friend by the hand, so we
can soar and roar together on this planet as
we both commemorate, elaborate, and
rejoice.

Yes, I can be a Tea Baker, Tea Maker, and so
much more.

Yes, I can because SABAOTH is my next
Open Door.
Yes, I can. Yes, I can.
I'm entitled to all
Yesses and Amens.

# Vine

Thy mother is like a vine in thy
blood, planted by the waters:
she was fruitful and full of
branches by reason of many waters.

**Ezekiel 19:10 KJV**

# A Natural Mom

She is my mom, but she isn't my mother,
Naturally.

She is a woman that nurtures natural
things, like a conglomerate family and
spiritual things, naturally given to her.

Naturally, she's against all negative words
someone has said that hurts another's
spirit.

Naturally, she is a teacher, not just an
educator, the kind that forbears with
patience who considers listening
with returns of an answer.

She tells your secrets only in prayer.
She's a SWEETY PIE MOTHER OF MINE,
her DNA epitomizes it.

Naturally, she sees you exceeding,
excelling in every imaginable thought that
comes to your mind.
Naturally, she's passionate about your
dreams, so please don't leave them behind
because EL QANNA reveals and
dispatches them in time.

She loves unconditionally
A Natural Mom

# Glorify

When He comes, in that Day, to be
glorified in His saints and to be
admired among all those who
believe, because our testimony
among you was believed.

## 2 Thessalonians 1:10 NKJV

# The One I Admire

The one I admire
You are the reason I am the person
that I am.
I admire you

I know it was challenging raising a
high-spirited child like me.
There were times when I acted like I didn't
appreciate you as a gift sent from the
FATHER above because of my unmannerly
conduct. Yet, your love never wavered.
I admire you

Watching your sacrifice and persistence of
diligent provisions by always having enough
to adeptly contribute in the accomplishments
and goals of your scion, offspring, loved ones.
I admire you

I admire you for a lot of things that only my
heart can speak. As I ponder priceless words
for you which
I have many more names.
LOVE, AFFECTIONATE, KINDHEARTED,
GRACIOUS, GENEROUS, CONSIDERATE
PRAYER WARRIOR,
I ADMIRE YOU, PRICELESSLY.

10.

# You

This is my commandment, that you
love one another,
as I have loved you.

**John 15:12 KJV**

# Tea Chapter 2
## Sisters
## Love One Another

# Beauty

Charm is deceitful and beauty is vain,
But a woman who fears (reverence)
the Lord, she shall be praised.
Give her of the fruit of her hands,
And let her own works praise her in
the gates.

**Proverbs 31:30-31 NKJV**

13.

# A Loving Woman She Conveys

A woman that constantly succors
considerably aids someone to achieve
extraordinary, unreachable possibilities.
One who shows empathy and is very
skillful in many things.
She's ready with open arms to give the
love that she has conveyed.
She shares her erudition without pride,
displaying a replica of herself, advocating
in a lady-like mannerism composure.
A woman of love that expresses it with
acts of generosity towards her neighbors
without delays.
A Kappa Coach, Preacher, Teacher,
Heroic Advisor who's presented with a
BOW LACE BUSHEL OF PEARTA POWDER
PERFUME SCENTED CARNATIONS
that Says from your
SOUL CORE STRINGS,
confidence is hers, ladies, to be chosen a
Golden Girl who's UNAFRAID to saunter
and ramble in the earth, establishing,
exhibiting her GOD-GIVEN talents!
Her heart that expresses love,
GOD's Love, She Conveys.

# Peace

Now may the God of peace who brought up our Lord Jesus from the dead, that great Shepherd of the sheep, through the blood of the everlasting covenant, make you complete in every good work to do His will, working in you what is well pleasing in His sight, through Jesus Christ, to whom be glory forever and ever. Amen.

**Hebrews 13:20-21 NKJV**

# She's a Pleasing Teava Deava

She's a pleasing Teava Deava who has been
given ten letters in her immediate name,
more or less, to complete a sentence.
She's a woman who often accepts the blame.
She's pleasing, attempting to placate and
appease everyone around her leaving her
name behind. A woman who loves without
reason, to everyone she greets,
she does the same. Even when it's selfless
acts with benevolence, guilty, or accused of
loving without a cause.
Someone who's determined no matter what
circumstances try to distract, hinder,
obstruct, inhibit, impede.
She's pleased with the right touch, warm
hands, and a compassionate heart to match.
She's like a sympathetic
FLOWERY BUDDY-SISTER
who empathetically takes a friend to visit
a loved one's residing resting place.
Even as she would delightfully give rides to
the voting polls, as well as to the grocery
store, or just having Tea Lunch at her
favorite Tea Café.
She's pleasing, appeasing inside and out, a
person who knows that EL-OLAM'S love
gives insight.
She's GOOD-NATURED, GOD-GIFTED,
ENTHUSIASTIC, and BLAZING.
She is a pleasing Deava.

16.

# Lead

Let sisterly love continue.

**Hebrews 13:1 KJV**

Tea Lady's Poetry of Love

# Sister to Sister

MACCADDESHEM, the Sanctifier,
created us to have emotions, feelings, and
intelligence. We as women have been
amid some of the same diverse hardships;
low self-esteem, insecurity, racism,
chauvinism,
portrayed as "less than" by society
while scandalizing our name.
But EL-GIBHOR has put us together to be
His Glory and man's favor.
Also, our children's faithful
confidant.
Just understand this, when we wrestle
with life's agonies, ordeals, burdens,
anguishes, spins, and journeys trying to
make a place in life's span time duration,
know your part is to nurture in nature's
whole human race.
So my sister, if you need an attentive lug,
or a word of prayer or a shoulder to lean
on, with no voice, I'm on STAT call for
any stratum of chitchatting.
Sister to Sister,
with the CREATOR,
there's a Room in the Inn.

18.

# Given

For God hath not given us the spirit
of fear; but of power, and of love,
and of a sound mind.

**2 Timothy 1:7 KJV**

# "Fear Not"

Teavas Ladies You can become a Fierce
Woman of YAHWEH-ROHI with flaws,
Strengths, and Weaknesses.
I encourage you, don't give up or give into
life's ultimatums or requests of
compromises. You can make a difference in
this Economy, Government, and Nation.
I will hold you up before ADONAI.
Be engaged, industrious, my sister.
Your purpose, destiny, and vision will come
to fruition. It is in the LORD's hands.
Hold on!
It will show that you have stood stout.
ROHI calls you
THE APPLE OF HIS EYE.
He promised to continue to watch over us
until He comes back for His
BEAUTIFUL EMORA PAINTED
PORTRAIT BRIDES.
He's pleading mercy, seeing faith and
victory over His PEARL GIRL DAUGHTERS,
having a lack of distress. Oh my dear sweet
ones, Hold on, Hold on. You're in winning
hands with the LORD, who's
the VICTORY VICTOR.
As an INVALUABLE EXQUISITE JADE STONE,
FEAR NOT!
To YAHWEH, the way of light.

# Sweetness

Ointment and perfume rejoice the heart: so doth the sweetness of a woman's friend by hearty counsel.

**Proverbs 27:9 KJV**

21.

# A Darling Tea Sister at Heart

She's a Sister at Heart.

She's like a best amiga
when she hugs you, you feel it.

When she Facetime you, you have no
need to put on your weave.

When she needs you, you'll be there.

Marriage or Loss of a loved one, my
HAZEL EYES SISTER-FRIEND, she is there to
hold your hand in a communion petition
plea to GOD for healing, wholeness,
restoration to your family and kindred
as well.

There's a special bond between the two,
who respects each other's point of view.

She will tell you when you look silly or
look gorgeous in your rhinestone
sharpshooter pointy toe shoes.
Face it, girl, She Loves You.
A Prized, Apple-Berry Beloved It,
Tea Sister at Heart

22.

# Winter

For, lo, the winter is past, the rain is
over and gone;
The flowers appear on the earth; the
time of the singing of birds is come,
and the voice of the turtle is heard
in our land;
The fig tree putteth forth her green
figs, and the vines with the tender
grape give a good smell.
Arise, my love, my fair one,
and come away.

**Song of Solomon 2:11-13 KJV**

# Tea Chapter 3

## The King's Garden Filled with Flowers for His Daughters

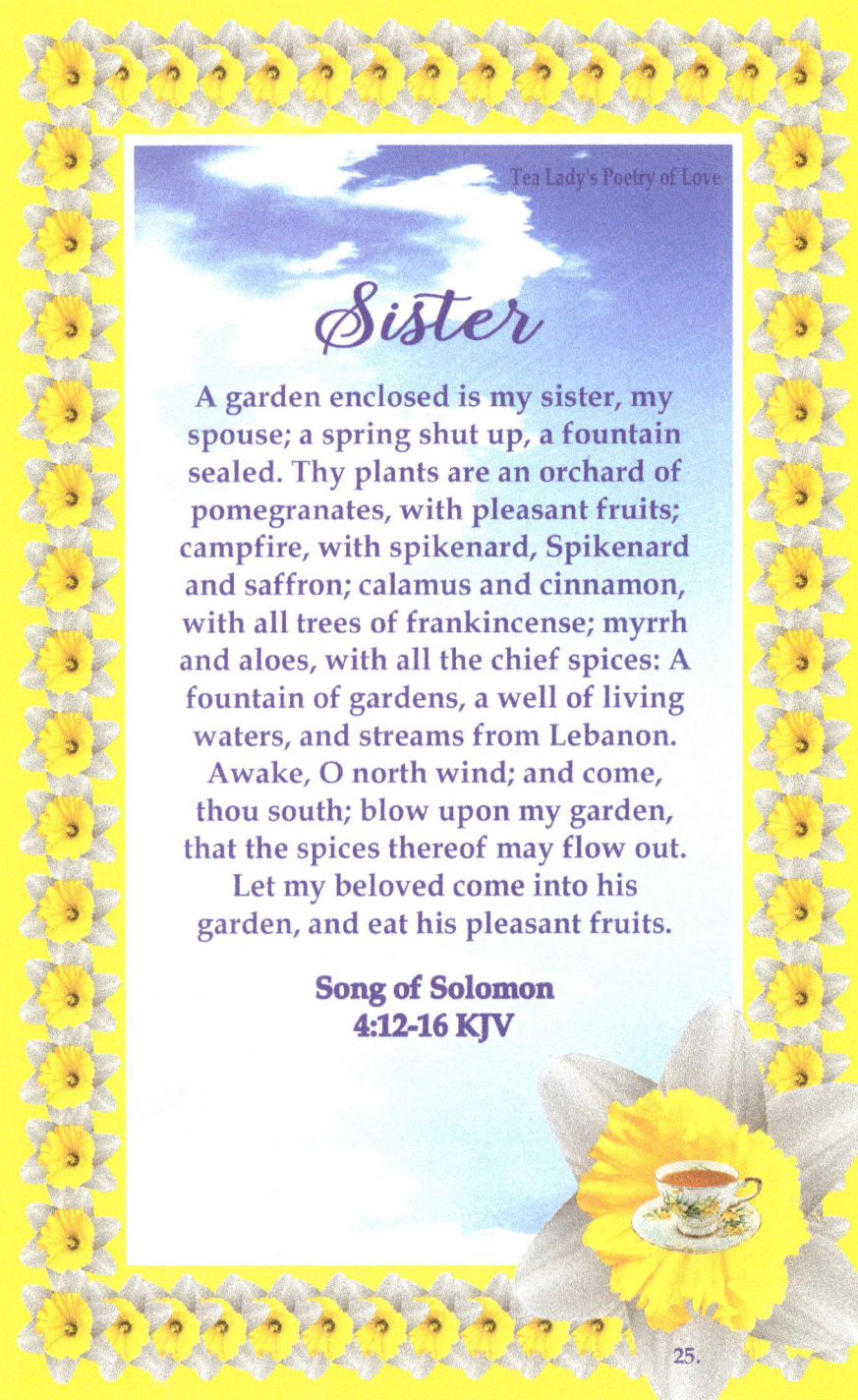

# Sister

A garden enclosed is my sister, my spouse; a spring shut up, a fountain sealed. Thy plants are an orchard of pomegranates, with pleasant fruits; campfire, with spikenard, Spikenard and saffron; calamus and cinnamon, with all trees of frankincense; myrrh and aloes, with all the chief spices: A fountain of gardens, a well of living waters, and streams from Lebanon. Awake, O north wind; and come, thou south; blow upon my garden, that the spices thereof may flow out. Let my beloved come into his garden, and eat his pleasant fruits.

**Song of Solomon
4:12-16 KJV**

# The King's Ivory Pearl
# Tea Garden

THE KING'S IVORY PEARL TEA GARDEN...
is full of life, laughter, love, flowers, fruits,
and filled with all kinds of bearing herbs.
ELOHIM blew a mist of refreshing water
from four parts of the earth with
tranquility in His peaceful, serene ocean
stream garden.
It's the most lovely garden that speaks of
His creative beauty in good-natured to all
grass, flowers, animals, trees, and the
whole human race. Saying, "you are mine."
THE KING'S GARDEN calls each flower by
"name" lovely,
pleasantly, splendid, inviting.
Their fragrances spread throughout
universes capturing loneliness, betrayal,
abandonment, and neglect.
Their leaves breathe verdure, jubilation,
vitality. They rejoice in sprightliness while
reviving and regenerating.
THE KING'S GARDEN will be full of fruit-
bearing seeds, spreading love, laughter,
and life that blossoms greeting of
effervescence in every season
from FATHER GOD above.

26.

# Pray

Call to me and I will answer you and
tell you great and unsearchable things
you do not know.

**Jeremiah 33:3 NIV**

Tea Lady's Poetry of Love

# MY PRAYER...

FATHER GOD

Kings Bow Before you,

so do I with a Humble

Heart and appreciation

with thanks to your

Glorious Majestic Majesty

Tea Gardens, full of love,

Gracias!

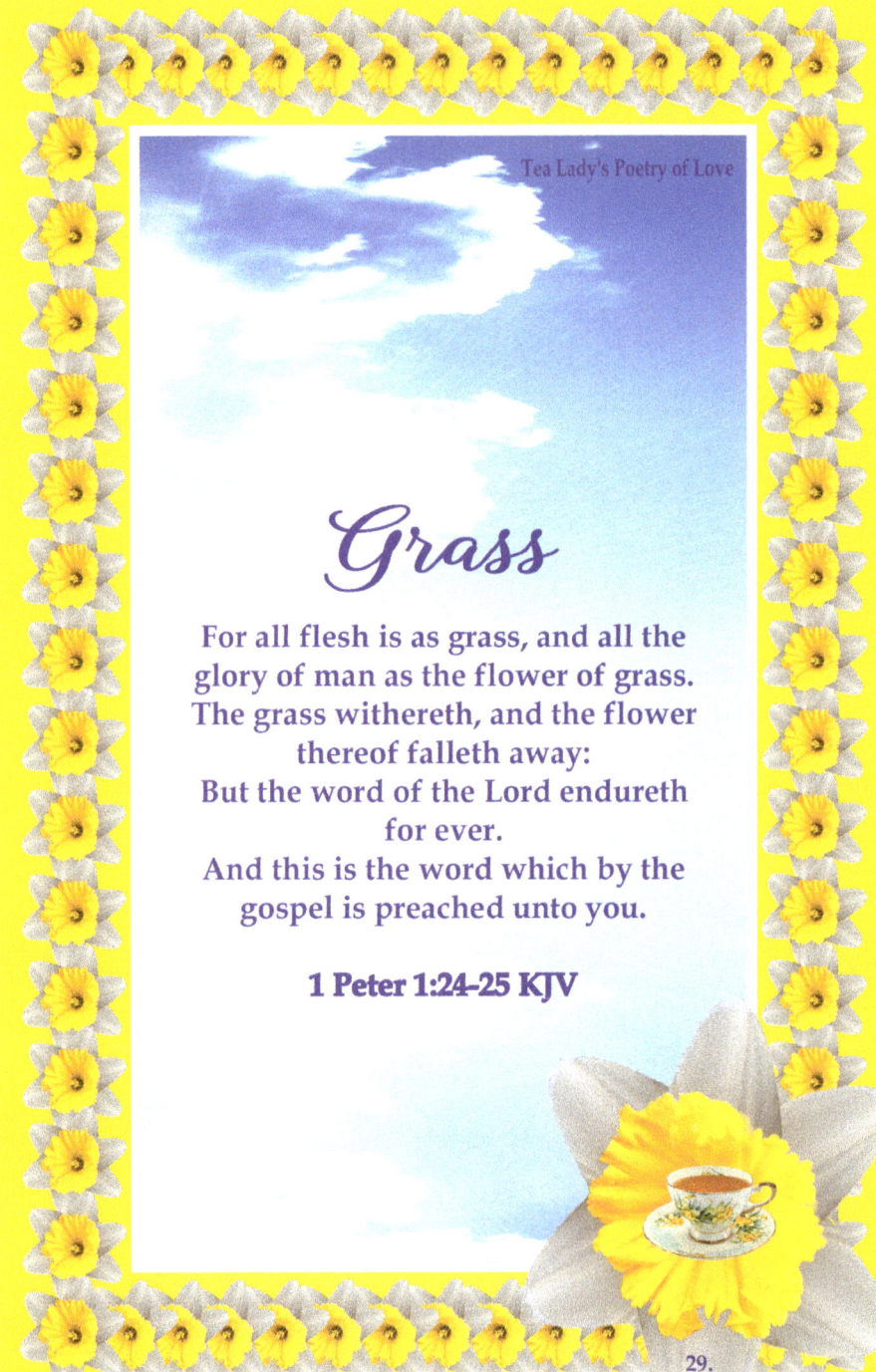

# Grass

For all flesh is as grass, and all the
glory of man as the flower of grass.
The grass withereth, and the flower
thereof falleth away:
But the word of the Lord endureth
for ever.
And this is the word which by the
gospel is preached unto you.

**1 Peter 1:24-25 KJV**

Tea Lady's Poetry of Love

# Flowers

Flowers have **no loss**.
They freely blossom gorgeously
in the SON OF DAVID'S
riveting, reinvigorating, ravishing
EVERGREEN GARDEN.
Each one speaks of his searchable,
loving-kindness, budding care.
So spend time in a lily field that
gives moments of quiet, peace,
serenity.
Take time to smell their rich sweet
aromas that are captivating,
charming like yesterday's
purple, red, orange, and
a yellow bouquet of bonnets sent to
you as a wedding gift
on a beautiful brisk
SUN SHINING DAY.

# Spirit

But we all, with open face
beholding as in a glass the glory of
the Lord, are changed into the same
image from glory to glory, even as
by the Spirit of the Lord.

**2 Corinthians 3:18 KJV**

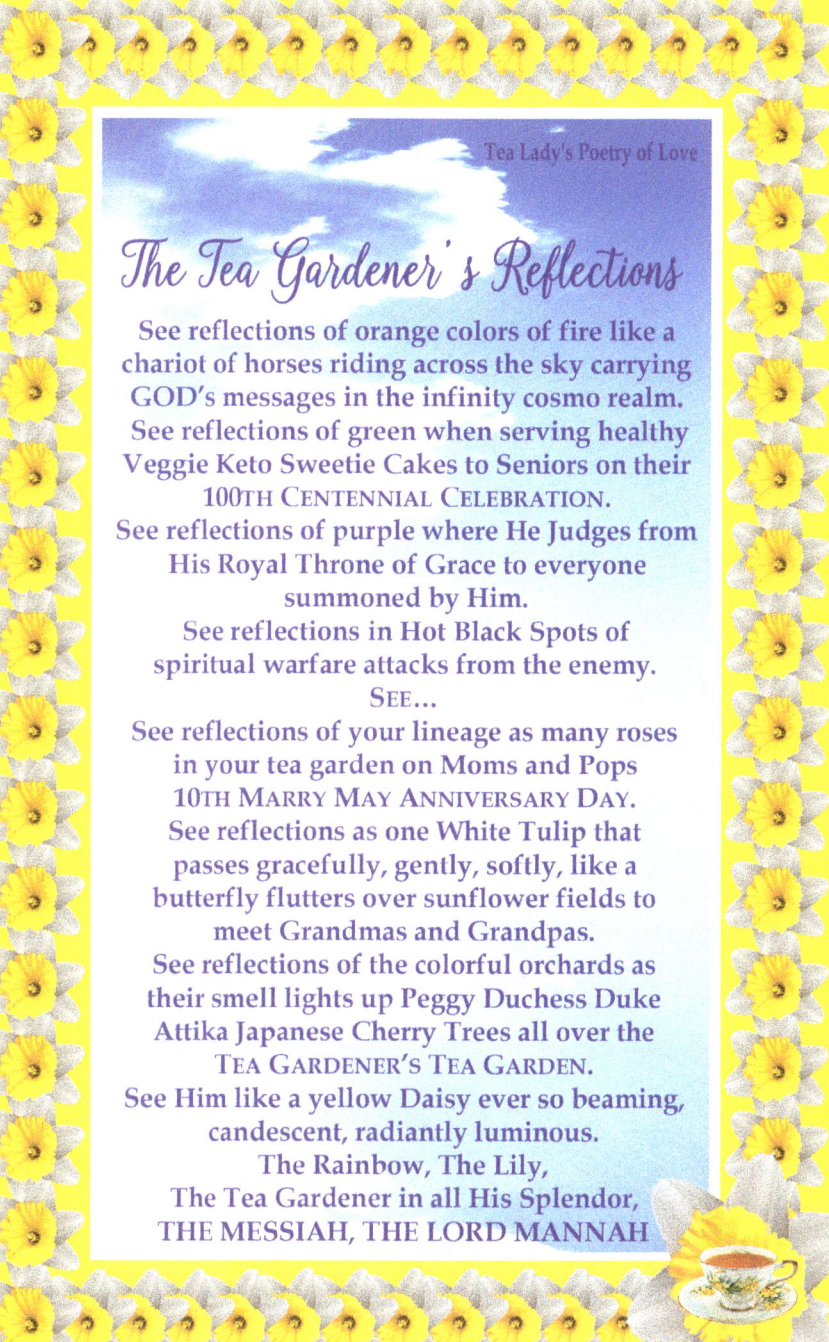

Tea Lady's Poetry of Love

# The Tea Gardener's Reflections

See reflections of orange colors of fire like a
chariot of horses riding across the sky carrying
GOD's messages in the infinity cosmo realm.
See reflections of green when serving healthy
Veggie Keto Sweetie Cakes to Seniors on their
100TH CENTENNIAL CELEBRATION.
See reflections of purple where He Judges from
His Royal Throne of Grace to everyone
summoned by Him.
See reflections in Hot Black Spots of
spiritual warfare attacks from the enemy.
SEE...
See reflections of your lineage as many roses
in your tea garden on Moms and Pops
10TH MARRY MAY ANNIVERSARY DAY.
See reflections as one White Tulip that
passes gracefully, gently, softly, like a
butterfly flutters over sunflower fields to
meet Grandmas and Grandpas.
See reflections of the colorful orchards as
their smell lights up Peggy Duchess Duke
Attika Japanese Cherry Trees all over the
TEA GARDENER'S TEA GARDEN.
See Him like a yellow Daisy ever so beaming,
candescent, radiantly luminous.
The Rainbow, The Lily,
The Tea Gardener in all His Splendor,
THE MESSIAH, THE LORD MANNAH

32.

# *Pray*

But I pray to you, Lord, in the time
of your favor; in your great love,
O God, answer me with your sure
salvation.

**Psalm 69:13 NIV**

# I AM PRAYER

I can keep your mind at ease,
providing the answer to all things.
I am prayer

I am more powerful, believable when
one hour of prayer is released in the
atmosphere.
I am prayer

Angels deliver the results of an answer
out of heaven above through the
TRUE VINE RESCUER.
I am prayer

I will manifest miraculously,
especially when two or more
are gathered in my Name.
I am Jesus PRAYER

Salvation comes
only one way called
by ME.
I AM JESUS

34.

# Pleasant

A pleasant thing it is for the
eyes to behold the
sun.
Because the sun hath
looked upon me.
Then shall
the righteous
shine forth as the sun.

**Ecclesiastes 11:7 KJV**

Tea Lady's Poetry of Love

# *Tea Garden's Sunlight*

TEA GARDEN'S SUNLIGHT...
helps flowers to grow. They come in a
variety of different colors, shapes, and
sizes.
Flowers don't just come to life in a
lovesome, radiant, resplendent flower pot.
It takes a lot of hard work and dedication
for them to become fully exuberant and
healthy.
It all begins with a tea seed.
Seeds have to be planted in a stable
environment to sustain proper growth.
SUNLIGHT gives to the tea seeds soil
extraordinary outstanding amounts
of nutrients.
SUNLIGHT reveals vision to the eyes to see
ELOHIM CHAYIM's GLORY in the tea
seed as a lovely site for flourishing.
SUNLIGHT heals broken hearts from a dark
week of misunderstandings.
SUNLIGHT brightens your personality to be
intrigued as a positive thinker.
SUNLIGHT repairs restore more elation to a
marriage that speaks; she's still the most
statuesque girl in his world.
SUNLIGHT is shared with an evening full of
prospects, potential capabilities in the
pursuit of happiness.

36.

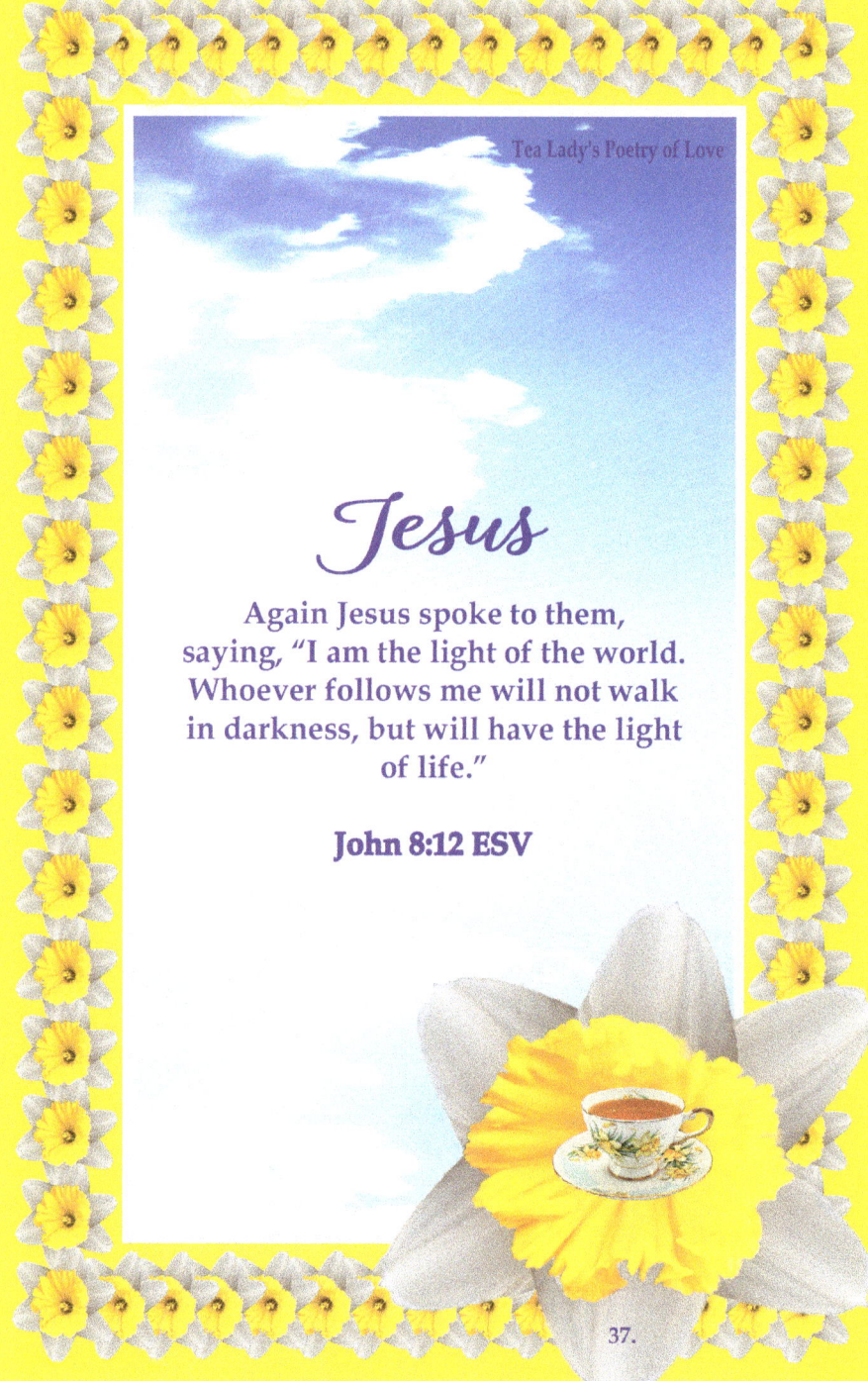

Tea Lady's Poetry of Love

# Jesus

Again Jesus spoke to them, saying, "I am the light of the world. Whoever follows me will not walk in darkness, but will have the light of life."

**John 8:12 ESV**

# Sprouting Tea Seeds

Sprouting tea seeds makes the WORD OF
GOD prosper when planted by every word
The HAKODESH, The COMFORTER,
The PARACLETE, The INTERCESSOR,
speaks into our lives.
Sprouting seeds grow into flawless poetry
of history that will thrive, develop for a
lifetime of never-ending stories.
Sprouting seeds will breed life concepts
to reality, like making school laws and
terms for each spring break to decide.
Sprouting seeds refers to the
undeferrable believer to welcomely
accept
His reclamation that marks life is ours to
guide, own, and reclaim.
Sprouting seeds grow in the house of
EMMANUEL to continue to walk in his
ways from birth.
Sprouting seeds impacts your spiritual
growth significantly among our
civilization in society.
Sprouting seeds have been cultivated by
sources of tea seeds for germination.
Sprouting seeds will prune out what is
not in GOD's definition.

Tea Lady's Poetry of Love

# Share

Do not forget to do good and to share with others, for with such sacrifices God is pleased.

**Hebrews 13:16 NIV**

39.

Tea Lady's Poetry of Love

# MY PRAYER...

FATHER GOD...
you are the sweetest taste
of Love to the Tea world.
I come asking you
for more Tea Blends
to share Sip Cups
with my Teava Sisters.

# Rose

I am the rose of Sharon, And the lily
of the valleys.
Like a lily among thorns, So is my
love among the daughters.

**Song of Solomon 2:1-2 NKJV**

Tea Lady's Poetry of Love

# Rose You

Are in all moments of celebrations.
Your RED RUBY BEAUTY changes my
visage to a smile when you enter a tea
room. You capture our advertence as your
presence romantically brightens up a
tea table.
RED RUBY,
You are infectious to everyone
that engages your
Red Ruby Aroma and Beauty.
You're jaunty, jubilant, full of love;
there's excitement when you are present.
I can feel your warmth,
RED RUBY.
I believe GOD'S GLORY has sealed each
one of your stems, which makes you
stand out above all the rest.
"ROSE" you are RED RUBY in Beauty.
Your beauty as a FLOWER effectuates
Winsome Daughters lavishing joy of
enjoyment to their ROSE BUSH TEA
GARDEN IN THE SPRINGTIME.
Rose, you are
RED RUBY IN YOUR BEAUTY.

Tea Lady's Poetry of Love

# Strengthen

The Lord will guide you
continually,
and satisfy your soul in drought,
and strengthen your bones;
You shall be like a watered garden,
and like a spring of water,
whose waters do not fail.

**Isaiah 58:11 NKJV**

43.

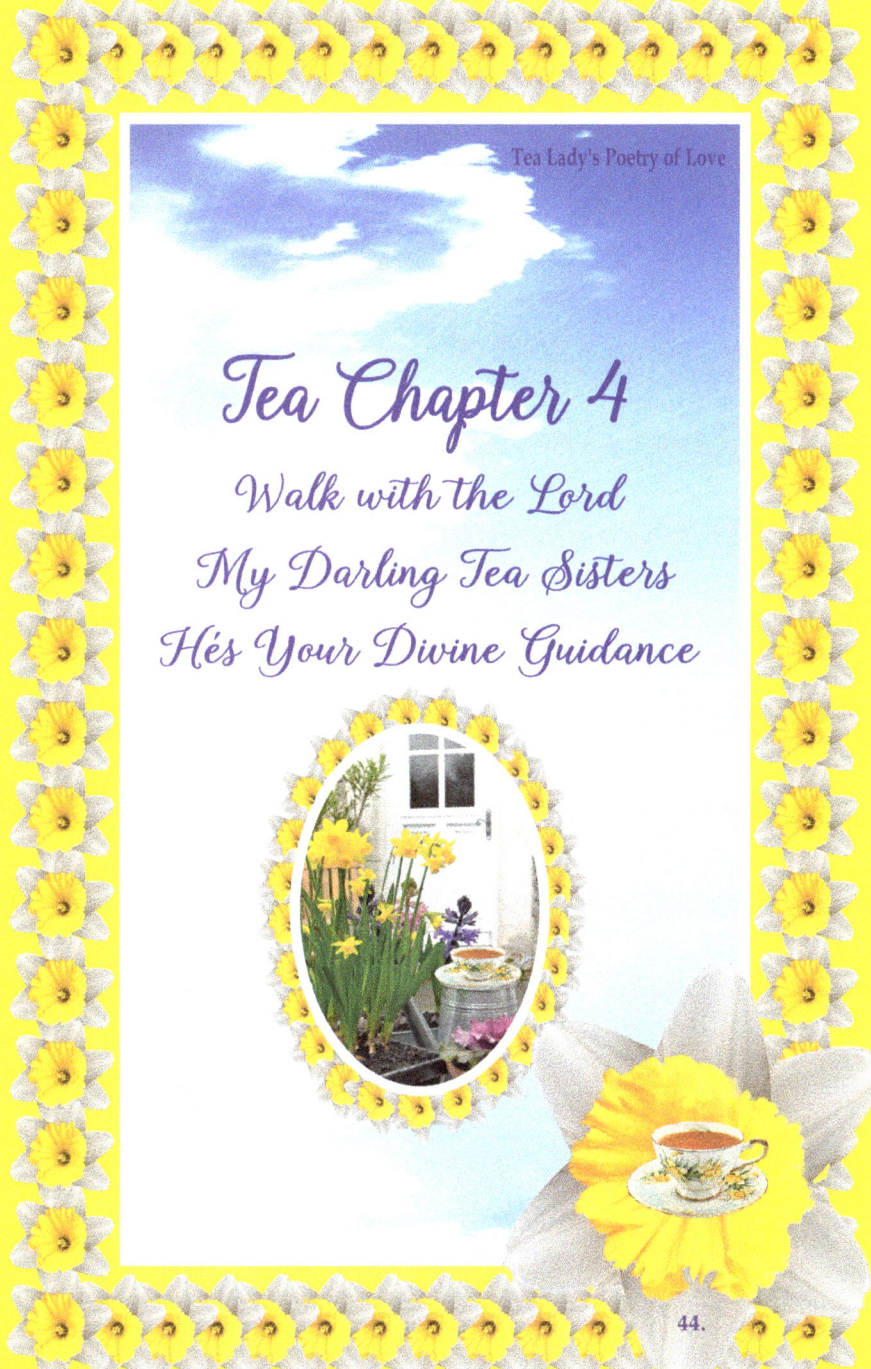

# Tea Chapter 4

## Walk with the Lord
## My Darling Tea Sisters
## He's Your Divine Guidance

# Visitation

Thou has granted me life and
favour, and thy visitation hath
preserved my spirit.
And these things has thou hid in
thine heart:
I know that this is with thee.

**Job 10:12–13 KJV**

45.

# Inner Heart

An inner heart needs to be nourished with
precious Teabit Nuggets of Jewels.
As a SISTER-SAVER, HONEYBUN-BLAZER,
STRAWBERRY BLONDE-STEAMER,
she's always ready to share Her
"PUNCTUAL GOLDEN PROMPT RULE."
The inner heart begets healing medicine to a
woman's reliance and credence.
So my Teava Sister, to allow your process to
begin, start taking each day a dose of
"I shall not lack."
A teaspoon of He makes me rest in a safe
nest filled with quietude and placidity that
calms me spiritually in stormy weather when
the waters are raging.
The next day take a full spoon of
"life will not overtake me,"
because His presence surrounds me,
His face will shine upon me as my relaxer.
Then the following day, apply
one dose daily of
I AM affirmed in my identity from
spiritual authority, with
the priest of destiny, and the peace of
righteousness — lastly, take a demitasse
teacup tasty taste of gentleness,
pleasantness, from all earthly tea leaves to be
rejuvenated, renewed, healed,
and restored.

Tea Lady's Poetry of Love

# Pray

Therefore I tell you, whatever you
ask for in prayer, believe that you
have received it, and it
will be yours.

**Mark 11:24 NIV**

47.

# MY PRAYER...

Heavenly Father...
Lord, I'm asking you to
pour down on your beloved
daughters a foundation
of living waters that
Springs forth an
overflow of your
wisdom.

48.

# Open

The eyes of the Lord are upon the
righteous, and His ears are open
unto their cry.

**Psalm 34:15 KJV**

# God's Eyes

No one is OMNISCIENT, OMNIPRESENT
like GOD is OMNIPOTENT. His eyelids are
over all global regions watching over our
weaknesses, becoming adequately stronger in
His strength, ability.
He keeps His consistency stretching,
wide, protracted, and elongated.
GOD sees you, Teavas, as a vanquishing
conqueror by the faithfulness commitment of
His covenant for you to upend bedlam
tribulations, disruptions.
Depend on Him, Trust in Him
to go to His next dimension for you.
Ensuring you guardianship by
HIS SHARPENED SHIELD OF PROTECTION.
No one can keep you from
falling, only GOD, my
Chocolate-Box Sisters.
So beseech Him, entreat Him,
Lean on Him
He's a GOD who delegates
HIS GOLDEN NUGGET WILL.
He's a GOD who remains true to
His promises.
Be sure to know He will keep you on a
perfectly straight pathway because no one
sees your future so transparently,
But GOD's eyes only.

# Beautiful

He hath made every thing beautiful
in his time: also he hath set the
world in their heart, so that no man
can find out the work that God
maketh from the
beginning to the end.

**Ecclesiastes 3:11 KJV**

# Present Redemption

There's no time like the present because
we know who holds eternity.
"GOD the FATHER"
He pulls down time into our presence
while He redeems mankind back to
PARADISE LESSONS.
We need His anointing flowing in our
lives to keep us attentive and vigilant.
His raptor hawks are gliding, watching out
for us on standby, as
He's reassembling, reconstructing,
redeveloping, reuniting
a strong nation that will hasten to the
agonizing moans of
CHRIST's OBEDIENCE
with indestructible, piercing trumpet
sounds of triumph with power and
persistence to crush the devil's head into
chains of bondage.
As He prepares our Castle Manor until we
meet up with Him at the BELLA BELL
HEAVENLY PEARLY GATES. He's the HOLY
and MIGHTY ONE, a GOVERNMENT with no
Patience with Sin on the rise.
HE'S GOD'S SON and MAN'S
REDEMPTION PRIZE.

# Heart

Sorrow is better than laughter: for
by the sadness of the countenance
the heart is made better.

**Ecclesiastes 7:3 KJV**

# Sadness Sees Within the Eye Gates

I SEE the sadness in your eyes,
JEHOVAH SHAMMAH has released
all your supplies.
He opened up His storage treasure box
to quicken and to renew your mind.
Ladies, meditate on His goodness so you
won't feel stressed with anxiety,
lonely with no disguise to hide.
SEE faith as a mountain of
ELOHIM CHASEDDI's countenance
to behold.
SEE love as security covering refuge,
Teavas, by the HOLY RIGHTEOUS
EXISTENCE BEINGS who fly as
Angelic Hosts below to deliver and to
satisfy your desires among
each one of you.
SEE patience as a sparkling diamond
glow, seraphic, Godlike, lovely entity.
SEE self-control as topazes, sapphires,
garnets that the heart storage cool.
See JESUS as REST
in all life's storms.

54.

# Hope

For I know the thoughts that I think toward you, saith the Lord, thoughts of peace, and not of evil, to give you an expected end.

**Jeremiah 29:11 KJV**

Those who hope in the Lord will renew their strength.

**Isaiah 40:31 NIV**

But after that the kindness and love of God our Saviour toward man appeared. That being justified by his grace, we should be made heirs according to the hope of eternal life.

**Titus 3:4,7 KJV**

Now may the God of hope fill you with all joy and peace in believing, that you may abound in hope by the power of the Holy Spirit.

**Romans 15:13 NKJV**

# Happiness

For we are saved by hope: but hope that is seen is not hope: for what a man seeth, why doth he yet hope for? But if we hope for that we see not, then do we with patience wait for it.

**Romans 8:24-25 KJV**

For the law made nothing perfect, but the bringing in of a better hope did; by the which we draw nigh unto God.

**Hebrews 7:19 KJV**

For we through the Spirit wait for the hope of righteousness by faith.

**Galatians 5:5 KJV**

Now faith is the substance of things hoped for, the evidence of things not seen.

**Hebrews 11:1 KJV**

56.

# Blessing

Blessed be the God and Father of
our Lord Jesus Christ, which
according to his abundant mercy
hath begotten us again unto a lively
hope by the resurrection of
Jesus Christ from the dead,
To an inheritance incorruptible, and
undefiled, and that fadeth not away,
reserved in heaven for you.

**1 Peter 1:3-4 KJV**

Tea Lady's Poetry of Love

# In God Teavas

In God's Vision
is JEHOVAH LORD EZER
always to a means

In GOD EMMANUEL,
there's hope, ambition,
the pretension to achieve our
dreams because God
is with us

In God
Teavas, he gives you a Destiny to
Pursue

In God,
You can Buttress all things because
he has Overpop, Underpop,
and Strengthened
You

# King

Give heed to the voice of my cry,
my King and my God, for to You
I will pray.

**Psalm 5:2 NKJV**

# Tea Chapter 5

## Listening for the Cry

# Measure

Take heed what ye hear: with what
measure ye mete, it shall be
measured to you: and unto you that
hear shall more be given.

**Mark 4:24 KJV**

# Chamber Hearts

I'm here, I'm here. Hello, is anyone
listening? Will anyone take me
seriously?
Can't anyone see me wasting away?
I need someone to listen to me.
NOW RIGHT NOW IT'S IMPORTANT
Just when I thought I would run out of
the energy of deficient thoughts, of
disagreements looking all around me.
I looked unto eternity for amiability,
neighborliness, amicableness,
sociableness.
There was a voice at my heart chambers.
A wonderful surprise, on-time visitor
speaks. Who is it? I asked?
Are you listening?
I need to know, are you listening?
And the voice on the other side
said, "It's me, ABEL,
the DON, the CAVALIER,
the GENTLEMAN, the POLISHED and
REFINED MAN who will never leave
you, who's here to open your ears to
hearken to my voice,
I'm listening."

# Pray

Then you will call on me and come
and pray to me, and I will listen to
you.

**Jeremiah 29:12 NIV**

# MY PRAYER...

FATHER
GOD...
I know you hear
our prayers, as I speak
in your ear,
I just want to say softly
your Love is
Virtually at Hand.

# Arise

Arise, cry out in the night: in the beginning of the watches pour out thine heart like water before the face of the Lord: lift up thy hands toward him for the life of thy young children, that faint for the hunger in the top of every street.

**Lamentations 2:19 KJV**

# Loneliness

There's a loud cry from the young and old
women affected by this unstable disease
called Loneliness.

Loneliness is an emotion that travels,
contaminating, poisoning the whole body
that lands in the heart, triggered in the
mind, to meditate on sorrowful pains.

Each day, women are dying from
loneliness, depression, oppression,
heartbreak, heart shake, or heartache.

Loneliness can be triggered by no human
contact of concerns, conflict of opinions, a
contest of attitudes, disappointments with
grief or disbelieving letters without
communication confidence in oneself to
shy away from others, and so much more
unbeneficial memories.

But there's TEAVA TEA NEWS at the
TEA LADY's TEA TALK TEA TABLE to learn
how to take possession of your thoughts.

Loneliness can be stabilized over a
Grand-Magnifico, Fantabulous
Tea Garden Brunch
with some Sweety Bud Teava Ladies and
sister-friends, having sisterly, wholesome
Tea Parties, sipping up to memorable,
engaging, uplifting compliments.

# Called

Seek ye the Lord while
he may be found, call ye
upon him while he is near:

**Isaiah 55:6 KJV**

# Seek the Lord

Seek the LORD; this is right, Teavas, in the sight of the LORD.

Seek the LORD's graciousness,
it's Tea Etiquette to sip and recite upon.

Seek the LORD; you will be able to overcome any outrage, outbreaks, and upheaval detriments with His dulcet, tasty, enjoyably felicitous taste of sweetness He has stirred up for you.

Seek the LORD, its freedom indeed, to succeed in every promise He has made to everyone who will believe and achieve in him.

Seek the LORD; you can stand sturdy, sinewy, burly stalwart, on your knees surmounting, dismantling, all perilous pernicious situations.

Seek the LORD, and open opportunities for transforming remarkable manifestations will be yours to take possession of.

Seek the LORD; it will bring completion in holiness to endure the fullness of His Joy.

# Rock

From the end of the earth I will cry
unto thee, when my heart is
overwhelmed: lead me to the rock
that is higher than I.

**Psalm 61:2 KJV**

# Cries in the Dark
# Oh My Sistah Sistah

Cries in the dark are sounds of rejection,
the hopelessness of thoughts that invades
some of us ordinary common folks.
Cries in the dark occur more often
than not.
Cries in the dark can have a captured
effect within any racial class, rank, or
status of the masses.
Cries in the dark evoke meditating
adverse trials of adversities.
Cries in the dark see no hope for
tomorrow's breakthroughs.
Cries in the dark can't stop weeping tears
that climb bens, peaks
mounts too high to discover.
Cries in the dark drown into overnight
failures, disappointing memories.
Cries in the dark mate with pain and
hurts from the past.
Our HEAVENLY FATHER's open cruet
catches each teardrop of forgiveness to lay
aside on your bedside before the sun
arises to fill the seals of hope again.
Oh my Sistah, Cries in the dark
are no more relevant to your
blue skies.

# Holy One

Behold, thou shalt call a nation that
thou knowest not, and nations that
knew not thee shall run unto thee
because of the Lord thy God, and
for the Holy One of Israel; for he
hath glorified thee.

**Isaiah 55:5 KJV**

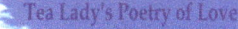

# Lady Lord Seekers

Ladies, the LORD is your SHEEPMAN who
keeps you from jealousy, envy, and strife.
He's the PILOT MASTER SHEPHERD that
should be your only desirable, satisfying,
gratifying delight.
So my sweet Sister of mine, arise on
His apprizing, remarkable, amazing
melody of waves,
take hold as a LADY LORD SEEKER.
Seeking your identity of success as a
lioness that roars in its own space to
conquer your uniquely
predestined Quest.
This will capture His heart with
pleasures as His voice calls your name.
MY LOVE, MY DOVE, thou art pleasing in
thou ways as a LADY LORD SEEKER.
Be acquiescence with sweetness; the rest
comes in time as a LADY LORD SEEKER.
So continue, my Sisters, as a Tea Sipper
that arrives on time for teatime as a
LADY LORD SEEKER.
GOD's presence will behold
His voice, listen softly as He speaks,
that shall not be erased because you are
marked as a LADY LORD SEEKER.
"Happy Bee Tea Hour"

# Pray

This is the confidence we have in approaching God: that if we ask anything according to his will, he hears us.

**1 John 5:14 NIV**

Tea Lady's Poetry of Love

# MY PRAYER...

FATHER
GOD...
teach me your ways.
So as the sun rises.
I can see your
Shekinah Glory
Shine
from up above.
It's my desire.

74.

# Shield

For the Lord God is a sun and
shield: the Lord will give grace
and glory.

**Psalm 84:11 KJV**

Tea Lady's Poetry of Love

# Sunshine

The sun has no light without CHRIST in
your atmosphere. He's the one who keeps
the sun shining recurrently in your
spectacle midnight drama scenes.
He has given resurrection power to see
you equipped, inured in all your weakest
appointed teabit times. If you pray to the
CONSOLATION of ISRAEL, He will
come
*through turmoil*        *through heartbreak*
Circumstances.
He's veracious to His word.
He knows all that you face.
No matter what comes, be assured
He's there to keep you buttoned-up,
snuggled up, and freed up from perils,
pitfalls, and predicaments.

Hold on to Him with all your fortitude,
courage, and durability.
He will see you prevail in each matter.
Just put your assertive poise in the
BREAD of LIFE and He will make
everything work out for your
UPRIGHT QUALITY, FINE ETHICAL,
TEA GREETS, GOOD DEEDS.

# Zion

Let the heaven and earth praise him,
the seas, and every thing that
moveth therein. For God will save
Zion, and will build the cities of
Judah: that they may dwell there,
and have it in possession. The seed
also of his servants shall inherit it:
and they that love his name shall
dwell therein.

**Psalm 69:34-36 KJV**

# Tea Chapter 6
## Let God
## Build it for You

Tea Lady's Poetry of Love

# *Plant*

And it shall come to pass, that like
as I have watched over them, to
pluck up, and to break down, and to
throw down, and to destroy, and to
afflict: so will I watch over them, to
build, and to plant, saith the Lord.

**Jeremiah 31:28 KJV**

79.

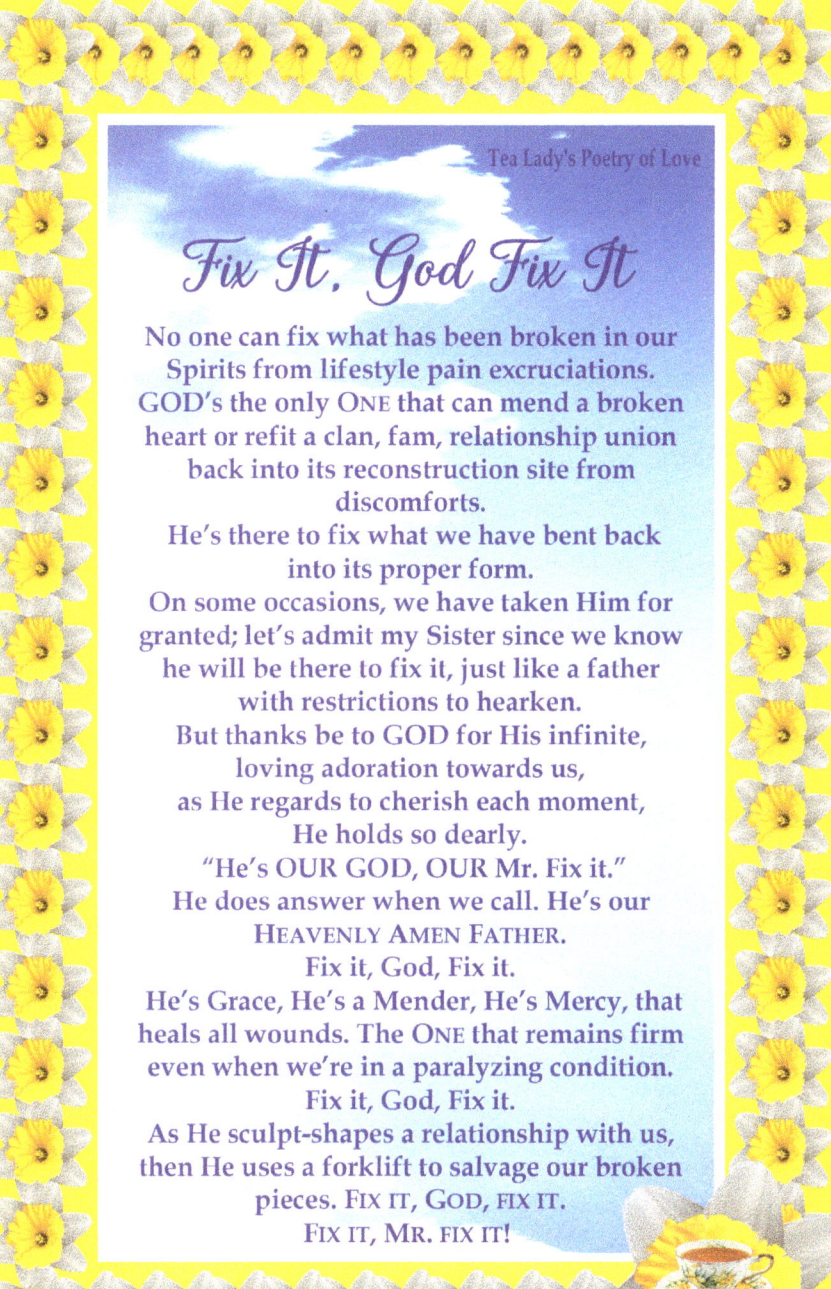

# Fix It, God Fix It

No one can fix what has been broken in our
Spirits from lifestyle pain excruciations.
GOD's the only ONE that can mend a broken
heart or refit a clan, fam, relationship union
back into its reconstruction site from
discomforts.
He's there to fix what we have bent back
into its proper form.
On some occasions, we have taken Him for
granted; let's admit my Sister since we know
he will be there to fix it, just like a father
with restrictions to hearken.
But thanks be to GOD for His infinite,
loving adoration towards us,
as He regards to cherish each moment,
He holds so dearly.
"He's OUR GOD, OUR Mr. Fix it."
He does answer when we call. He's our
HEAVENLY AMEN FATHER.
Fix it, God, Fix it.
He's Grace, He's a Mender, He's Mercy, that
heals all wounds. The ONE that remains firm
even when we're in a paralyzing condition.
Fix it, God, Fix it.
As He sculpt-shapes a relationship with us,
then He uses a forklift to salvage our broken
pieces. FIX IT, GOD, FIX IT.
FIX IT, MR. FIX IT!

80.

# Grace

According to the grace of God
which is given unto me, as a wise
master builder, I have laid the
foundation, and another buildeth
thereon. But let every man take
heed how he buildeth thereupon.
For other foundation can no man lay
that is laid, which is Jesus Christ.

**1 Corinthians 3:10–11 KJV**

# Master Builder

Some men build houses because A GIFT WAS
GIVEN TO THEM, but GOD creates them
because He's the CREATOR
CONDUCTOR, CONSTRUCTOR
of everything.
He's the master builder, I tell you
who has all the architectural plans in his
SEED Mouth to land.
He laid layers and layers of clay
in the sand, creating THE FIRST
ADAM called man IN HIS IMAGE and
LIKENESS because He Sovereignly Ably can.
He spoke to his creation and all creative
LIVING BEINGS, saying LET there BE, and
they obeyed His commands.
I tell you this, He's the master builder.
His blueprints were written without ink
which declares all things are possible for a
man to promulgate.
I tell you this He's the master builder;
with His Footsteps, He Leads man,
with His Handprints, He Guides man.
He keeps a sword in his mouth as a shield for
the WORD OF GOD to edify, to enlighten, and
to educate a man to be ready to build and able
to stand. I tell you this,
He's GOD the CREATOR.
THE MASTER BUILDER.

82.

# God

For every house is built by someone,
but the builder of all things is God.

**Hebrews 3:4 NASB**

# MY PRAYER...

FATHER GOD...
you are the master
builder for us to
exemplify.
Hold my hands
guide my feet so I can
remain forcible
puissant.

# Watch

I will stand upon my watch, and set me upon the tower, and will watch to see what he will say unto me, and what I shall answer when I am reproved.

**Habakkuk 2:1 KJV**

# I'M SITTING ON TOP OF THE WORLD

## WATCHING
## STANDING
## HANDLING
## DELIVERING
## SAVING
## PROVIDING
## HEALING
## WAVING MY BANNER FOR ALL
## TO BELIEVE IN MY ECHO!
## YAHWEH-NISSI

The Lord our banner. The Lord gives us the victory in spiritual warfare. When the enemy comes in like a flood, the Lord raises a banner of His love over us and covers us. He wages war on our behalf and makes us more than conquerors in Christ Jesus.
Exodus 17:15

# Child

Train up a child in the way he
should go; even when he is old he
will not depart from it.

**Proverbs 22:6 ESV**

# A Tea Mother's Tea Praise

Mother,
you are a faithful, loyal, trustworthy unique friend; this is true.
You are our TREASURED GOLD OF LIGHT on the earth, that's you!
We glean EL DE'OT's WORDS, the GOD OF KNOWLEDGE, of life truths, where bright illuminating blessings over showers you.
Having taught us how to treat others, that has been your lifestyle, exemplifying example too.
As becoming loving fathers and mothers to our children, that's a gift from you.
Teaching us to respect EL DE'OT's WORD and being Godly men, women, and helpmates too.
We owe these gifts GOD has given us unto you.
OUR ROCK, ONE OF A KIND,
RARE JEWEL GODSEND MOMMA MODEL,
We pour our appreciativeness praise of gratitude from our Tea kettle pot to your Teacup for being a TEA QUEEN.
Yes, for sure, you have been
a LIFE-GIVER, a LIFE-CHANGER,
a TEA WORLD SHAKER, and a TEATIME MAKER to others, as well as to your family as a GOODY TWO SHOES MOM TOO.

Tea Lady's Poetry of Love

# Pray

Rejoice always, pray continually,
give thanks in all circumstances; for
this is God's will for you in
Christ Jesus.

**1 Thessalonians 5:16-18 NIV**

89.

# I AM PRAYER

I am the mediator between GOD and
mortal humanity.
I am prayer

I will teach and show you my
characteristics, how to love the LORD THY
GOD and your neighbor every footstep you
take.
I am prayer

I move mountains and diffuse discord,
turmoil, unsettlement of pandemonium,
confusion in all surrounding environments
that hoovers destruction.
I am prayer

I mend families, save loved ones, and bring
children back home in their individuality.
I am prayer

I can heal the sick, comfort, relieve, and
salvage the broken-hearted.
I am Jesus PRAYER

I can change an atheist's belief and draw a
backslider into JEHOVAH's Mercy.
I AM JESUS

# Love

Love is patient, love is kind.
It does not envy, it does not boast,
it is not proud. It does not dishonor
others, it is not self-seeking, it is not
easily angered, it keeps no record of
wrongs.
Do everything in love.

**1 Corinthians 13:4-5, 16:14 NIV**

Tea Lady's Poetry of Love

# Tea Chapter 7

# Baby Love

Tea Lady's Poetry of Love

# Place

People were also bringing babies to
Jesus for him to place his hands on
them. When the disciples saw this,
they corrected them.
But Jesus called the children to him
and said, "Let the little children
come to me,
and do not hinder them, for the
kingdom of
God belongs to such as these.

**Luke 18:15-16 NIV**

93.

# Baby Love

Who has granted us to be the blessing
Carrier of you
BABY LOVE

Who has been mindful of us to allow us
to be willed your upraising
BABY LOVE

Who will train us how to love and teach
you to know GOD's will
BABY LOVE

Who will guide and trust us to be a part of
EL-OLAM'S wonderful plan in your life
BABY LOVE

Who has designed you to become
A VIRTUOUS WOMAN or A GOD-FEARING
MAN
BABY LOVE

YES YOU
Oh, how I pray EL-CHUWL'S empyrean
sanctified hand will stay
UPON BABY LOVE
IT'S YOU!

# Pray

Grandchildren are the crowning glory of the aged; parents are the pride of their children.

**Proverbs 17:6 NLT**

# MY PRAYER...

FATHER GOD
continue to
let your face
and grace behold my
grandchildren's
destiny.

# Girly Girls

Father God, may your hand
continually rest upon my
Granddaughter
who you have sent her as a gift
unwrapped from above to be a
TEA CHEERLEADER for
TEAVA GIRLS TO SERVE UP JOY,
FUN, at TEA PARTIES, that
REJUVENATES FRIENDSHIPS
AROUND
the Global Tea World.

# Grandmom's Daya Tea Girly Poem

It's been a long time coming.
Your kitty smile was worth it all.
You captured my heart as you snuggled and
wobbled with hugs under Grandmom's
arms.
That's why I call you Daya,
which means LIFE IN GOD, to teach you to
be an Angel Girl, to pray and share in others'
lives with a baby's breath, to be respectful,
to be grateful for your family showing you
how to love and grow into a
TEAVA GIRL SERVANT.
So have a long
life with tea parties, tea treats,
teddy bears, friends like on Sesame
Street; Big Bird, Ernie, Bert, and
tea cookies so sweet.
Daya, always remember to keep your
sunshine in a tea room with those big brown
eyes that sees truth.
You're truly Daddy's Little Baby Lady
Princess and
Mommy's Sweetheart too but
You'll always be Grandmom's special
KITTY GIRL,
my SWEETY GIRLY MEMORABLE
NAME just for you.

98.

# Perfect

Every good gift and every perfect gift
is from above, and cometh down from
the Father of lights, with whom is no
variableness, neither shadow of
turning. Of his own will begat he us
with the word of truth, that we should
be a kind of first fruits
of his creatures.

**James 1:17-18 KJV**

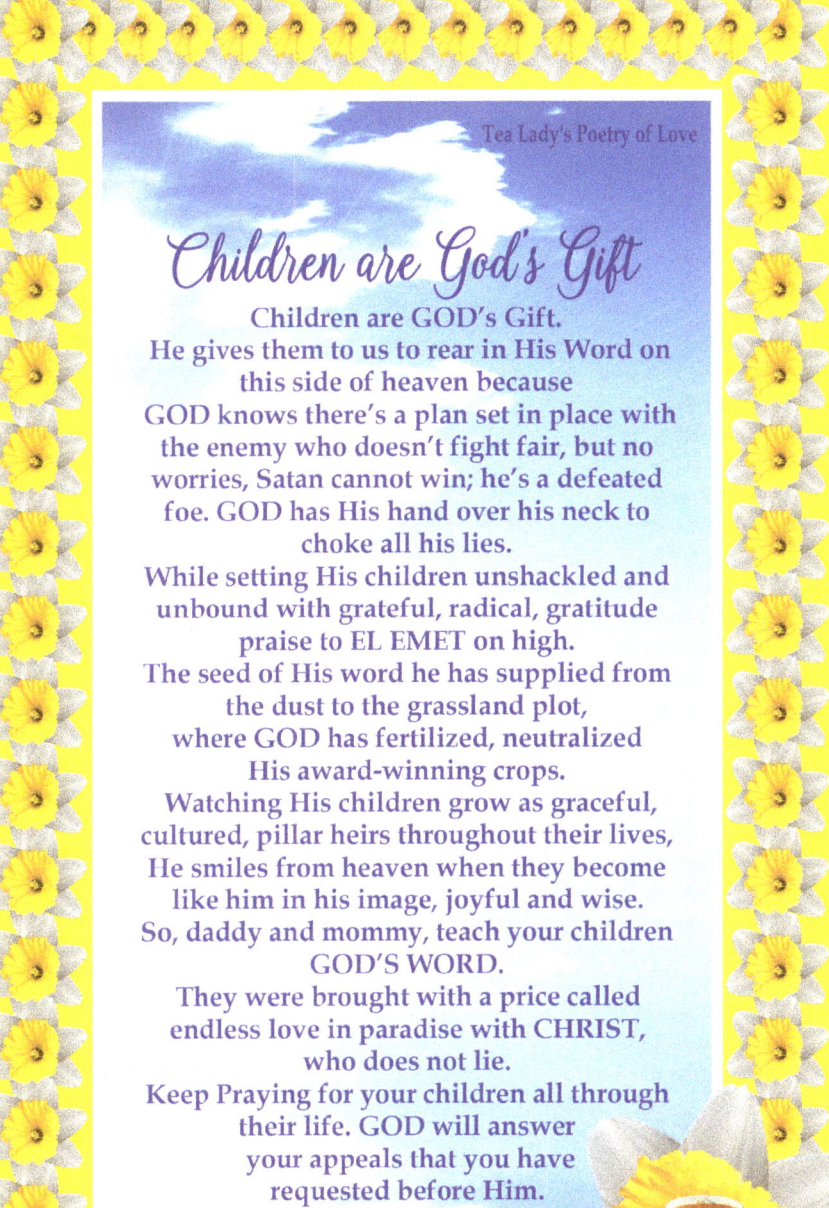

# Children are God's Gift

Children are GOD's Gift.
He gives them to us to rear in His Word on
this side of heaven because
GOD knows there's a plan set in place with
the enemy who doesn't fight fair, but no
worries, Satan cannot win; he's a defeated
foe. GOD has His hand over his neck to
choke all his lies.
While setting His children unshackled and
unbound with grateful, radical, gratitude
praise to EL EMET on high.
The seed of His word he has supplied from
the dust to the grassland plot,
where GOD has fertilized, neutralized
His award-winning crops.
Watching His children grow as graceful,
cultured, pillar heirs throughout their lives,
He smiles from heaven when they become
like him in his image, joyful and wise.
So, daddy and mommy, teach your children
GOD'S WORD.
They were brought with a price called
endless love in paradise with CHRIST,
who does not lie.
Keep Praying for your children all through
their life. GOD will answer
your appeals that you have
requested before Him.

# Fruit

For the seed shall be prosperous; the vine shall give her fruit, and the ground shall give her increase, and the heavens shall give their dew; and I will cause the remnant of this people to possess all these things.

**Zechariah 8:12 KJV**

I will sing for the one I love
a song about his vineyard:
My loved one had a vineyard
on a fertile hillside. He dug it up and cleared it of stones and planted it with the choicest vines.

**Isaiah 5:1-2 NIV**

But now that you have been set free from sin and have become slaves of God, the benefit you reap leads to holiness, and the result is eternal life.

**Romans 6:22 NIV**

# Seed

Children are a heritage from the Lord,
offspring a reward from him.
Like arrows in the hands of a warrior
are children born in one's youth. Blessed
is the man whose quiver is full of them.
They will not be put to shame when they
contend with their opponents in court.

**Psalm 127:3-5 NIV**

You shall eat the fruit of the labor of your
hands; you shall be blessed, and it shall be
well with you. Your wife will be like a
fruitful vine within your house; your
children will be like olive shoots around
your table.

**Psalm 128:2-3 ESV**

Children, obey your parents in everything,
for this pleases the Lord.

**Colossians 3:20 NIV**

# Sara

Through faith also Sara herself received strength to conceive seed, and was delivered of a child when she was past age, because she judged him faithful who had promised.

**Hebrews 11:11 KJV**

# WHO KNOWS

Who knows where a child comes from?
They're not from the stork's fairy tale story
that brings a newborn baby to parents
desiring a child or the make-believe tale of
joining together birds and the blessing bees.
Yes, they come from a seed so small that has
been cultivated before the beginning of
time.
This seed was first started when
FATHER GOD created society at large and
spoke seed would be ours to rear and to raise
in HIS HOPE HARVEST KINGDOM,
as He saw our need to replenish the earth
and to possess dominion.
He then placed the seed in two parent's
thoughts and desires, he called male and
female, which GOD created according to his
will. Yet all the more, He's Heavenly
delighted when a seed is conceived
according to His plan because that seed is in
a circular path motion, preparing to become
phenomenal in His wonderous, halcyon,
palmy, fertile land. This will allow the seed
to produce fresh organic fruit that keeps
multiplying while
passed down to
generations.

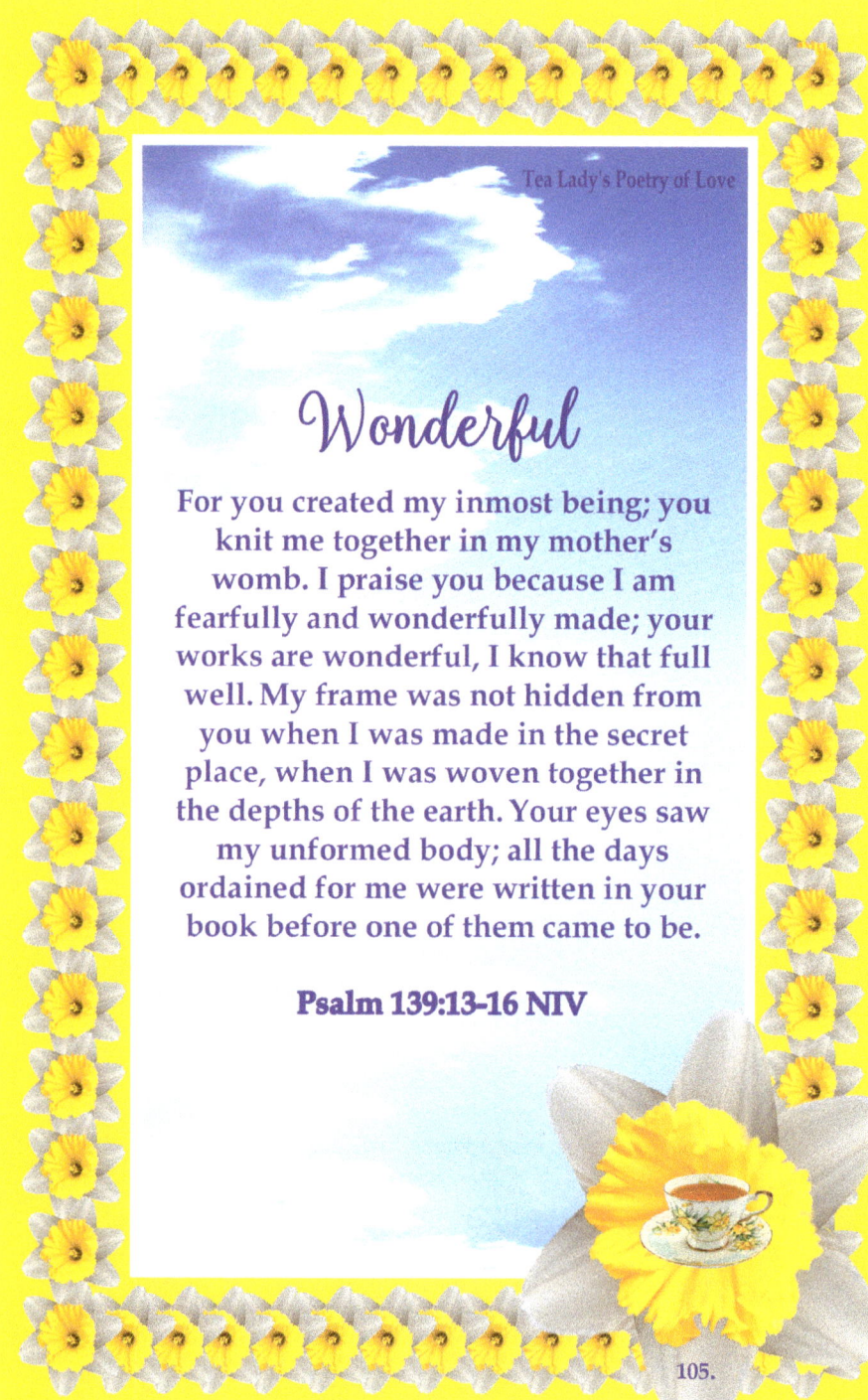

# Wonderful

For you created my inmost being; you knit me together in my mother's womb. I praise you because I am fearfully and wonderfully made; your works are wonderful, I know that full well. My frame was not hidden from you when I was made in the secret place, when I was woven together in the depths of the earth. Your eyes saw my unformed body; all the days ordained for me were written in your book before one of them came to be.

**Psalm 139:13-16 NIV**

# Over Showering King D's Seed
## Grandmom's Poem

GOD planted a seed in the eyes of a child,
King Dorrell, that you will see beyond your
imaginations. He planted a seed in the mind
of a child who was ordained to be in the
IMAGE OF HIM. He planted a seed in the heart
of a child who will look into the KINGDOM OF
GOD knowing he's Destin' to be a King.
Oh, my Happy Jaws Grandson, I'm so jolly
pleasantly pleased that GOD got involved.
He gave water that brought a patient sunny-
delight while your Mommy Nita's seed was
flourishing inside of her precious womb.
As Daddy Dorrell held her hand in the baby's
receiving room, he can't wait until Mommy
can make twisty baby locks out of your bushy
black full head of hair like Daddy locks.
"HIS FIRST BORN, HIS SON,"
He was right there with holding arms to take
diaper care of you. As he saw you drooling,
bubbly breath from your little puffy buffy
muscle baby chest. Then, as you arrived
home, it was such a gleeful, happy, jovial,
sightful family moment to see you wrapped
in your baby bear blankie, knitted just for
you. Oh my, Happy Jaws, Grandson, your
eyes were inquisitive, a pleasant espy scene
to behold, so kingly, regally like
Grandmommies and Grandpoppies dreamed
they would be.

# Reward

Lo, children are an heritage of the
Lord: and the fruit of the womb is
his reward.

**Psalm 127:3 KJV**

# A Bless Child

Children are a blessing from GOD.
They are cherishable progeny treasures that
share an abundance of CHRIST's fruit-
bearings that come with ups and downs
while enjoying all the turnarounds their
lives hold.
When GOD gives you a child, you are a
nurturing steward of his offspring.
Children have different personalities.
Each one is special in its own unique design.
Their ways can be perceived as a burden
sometimes, but just always remember to
believe they are a blessing from
EL-DEAH, The GOD OF WISDOM.
Children can do things that may upset your
pressure and mindset, but it's your
responsibility to correct them and never stop
giving affectionate love that comes from the
heart.
As time settles, they bring moments of
euphoria, pleasurable gladness, with
contentment as a reward of comfort.
This amount of love you give will definitely
affect the momentous time you spend
loving them.
Never take it for granted.
Your blessed child is a blessing
from EL-DEAH.

# *Be*

Because she hath set her love upon
me, therefore will I deliver her:
I will set her on high, because she
hath known my name.

**Psalm 91:14 KJV**

# Watch for Love

"From the depths of my heart, I love you."
Some write it, some say it, but who really
means it?
In a stable, caring, safe-side home, a
guardian can mean it towards their child.
A spouse can mean it towards their mate.
Likewise, a sibling can express it towards
another sibling.
It's purified, refined, unblemished,
untarnished, untainted when it comes
from the inner soul's depths where true
love never fails.
It comes from the heart that speaks
candidly when you allow EL SHADDAI,
GOD ALMIGHTY to come aboard.
Watch for Love.
It travels in a plethora of harmony,
tranquility, and serenity only
He can give so that we can provide safety,
security, stability to others.
"An enliven healthy, vibrant, thriving
heart is a tender, loving, caring,
sharing heart!"

110.

# *Eyes*

Therefore you shall lay up these
words of mine heart and in your
soul, and bind them as a sign on
your hand, and they shall be as
frontlets between your eyes.

**Deuteronomy 11:18 KJV**

Tea Lady's Poetry of Love

# Tea Chapter 8
## She Captured His Heart

*Her song of melody*

*" Let Freedom Ring "*

In him and through faith in him we may approach God with freedom and confidence.

**Ephesians 3:12 NIV**

# She

She possesses the ability to genuinely say to
another woman,
"I admire your qualities and attributes."
She is willing to share her talents to inspire.
She consoles even when she's hurting.
She-She learns from her mistakes and
acknowledges that she again is not perfect.
Her mouth has no malice, nor is it
destructive. Her smile remains unshaken.
She-She lifts her head and continues to walk
in the midst of mayhem.
She-She teaches the lives of a multitude,
illustrated, demonstrated from her life
experience.
She smiles with the reverence of
the LORD as her companion.
When her tears fall, she prays.
She has courage for the weak.
She's humble enough to say I forgive you
and to surrender.
She walks in self-assuredness with herself
without a need to prove it.
She proclaims with boldness and confidence
in her GOD.
She values her self-worth as a
testament testimony.
She's a PURE EMERALD PRECIOUS JEWEL.
She is not pretentious, but instead,
she presents herself as
She Is…..

Tea Lady's Poetry of Love

# Understanding

And I will give you pastors according to mine heart, which shall feed you with knowledge and understanding.

**Jeremiah 3:15 KJV**

115.

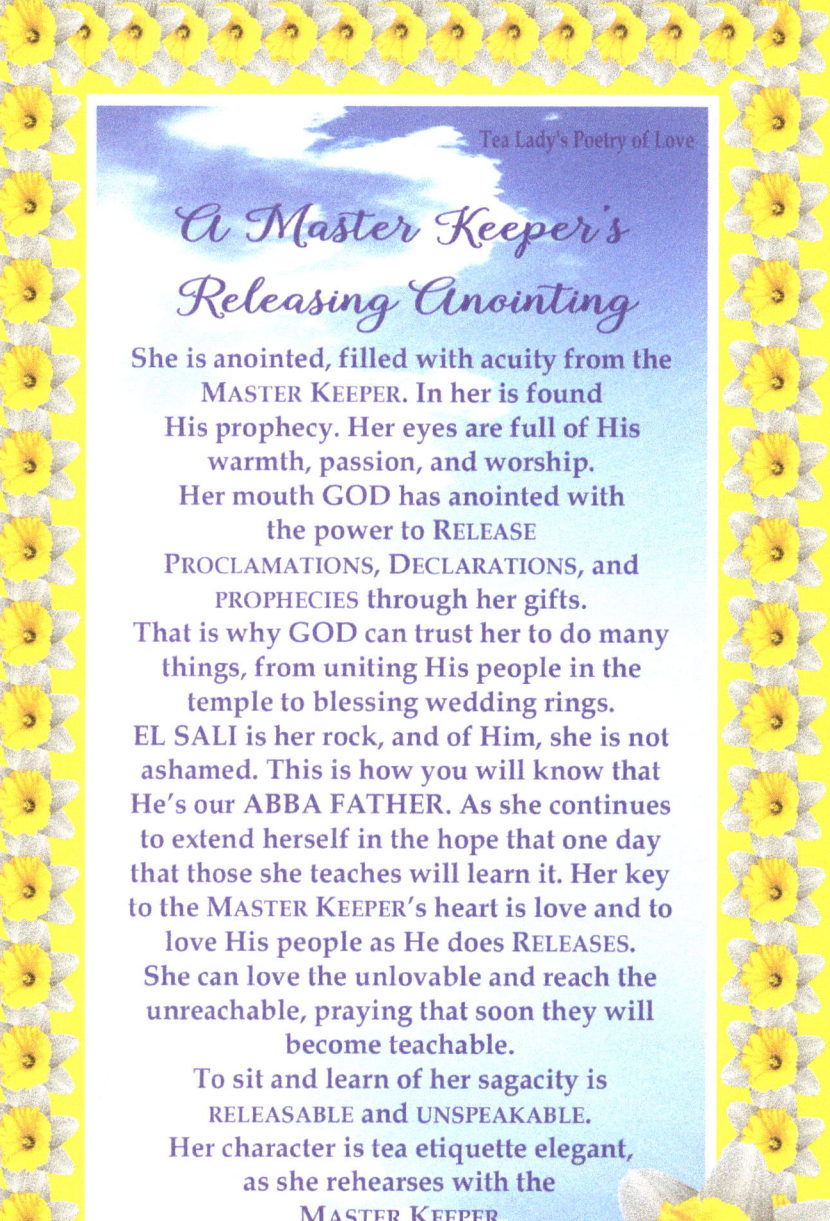

# A Master Keeper's Releasing Anointing

She is anointed, filled with acuity from the
MASTER KEEPER. In her is found
His prophecy. Her eyes are full of His
warmth, passion, and worship.
Her mouth GOD has anointed with
the power to RELEASE
PROCLAMATIONS, DECLARATIONS, and
PROPHECIES through her gifts.
That is why GOD can trust her to do many
things, from uniting His people in the
temple to blessing wedding rings.
EL SALI is her rock, and of Him, she is not
ashamed. This is how you will know that
He's our ABBA FATHER. As she continues
to extend herself in the hope that one day
that those she teaches will learn it. Her key
to the MASTER KEEPER's heart is love and to
love His people as He does RELEASES.
She can love the unlovable and reach the
unreachable, praying that soon they will
become teachable.
To sit and learn of her sagacity is
RELEASABLE and UNSPEAKABLE.
Her character is tea etiquette elegant,
as she rehearses with the
MASTER KEEPER.

# Direct

Direct your heart into the
Love of GOD.

**2 Thessalonians 3:5 KJV**

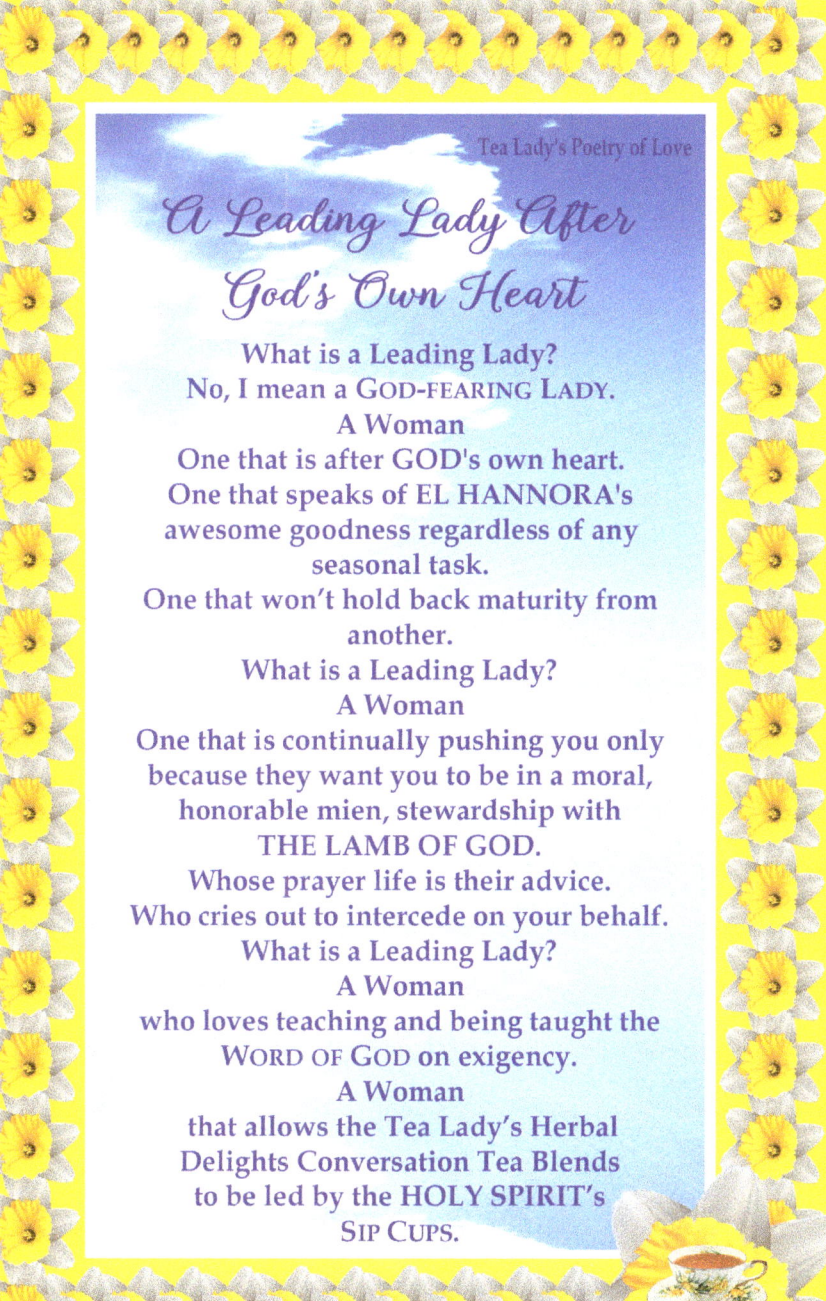

# A Leading Lady After God's Own Heart

What is a Leading Lady?
No, I mean a GOD-FEARING LADY.
A Woman
One that is after GOD's own heart.
One that speaks of EL HANNORA's
awesome goodness regardless of any
seasonal task.
One that won't hold back maturity from
another.
What is a Leading Lady?
A Woman
One that is continually pushing you only
because they want you to be in a moral,
honorable mien, stewardship with
THE LAMB OF GOD.
Whose prayer life is their advice.
Who cries out to intercede on your behalf.
What is a Leading Lady?
A Woman
who loves teaching and being taught the
WORD OF GOD on exigency.
A Woman
that allows the Tea Lady's Herbal
Delights Conversation Tea Blends
to be led by the HOLY SPIRIT's
SIP CUPS.

118.

# Lord

The Lord hath appeared of old unto
me, saying, Yea, I have loved thee
with an everlasting love: therefore
with loving kindness
have I drawn thee.

**Jeremiah 31:3 KJV**

# Agape Love

Agape Love
You keep me healed, happy, and whole.
I know I don't deserve to be called your
own, but thank you for looking beyond
all my imperfections and insecurities.
In you, ELOAH is where I can unite and
embrace my spirit with yours.
You keep me healed, happy, and whole.
You are my secret dwelling habitation
where I can abide and go hide in times of
distress, pestilence, and uncertainties.
I have found completion in your rest,
which gives the solace reassurance of love
and acquaintance of your stature.
Seeing your agape love hiding behind
every scene, waiting to make your
entrance known, showing your agape love
in all my situations.
You keep me healed, happy, and whole.
ELOAH's strapping one, I can hold,
who knows no fear, no defeat, and who's
not capable of deceit.
I desire more of your
Agape Love.

# Abide

And now abide faith, hope, love,
these three; but the greatest of
these is love.

**I Corinthians 13:13 NKJV**

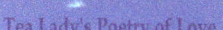
Tea Lady's Poetry of Love

# Love Is

Love is sending a GOD-MAN that
mediated as a witness for righteousness
sake.
Love is shedding His sinless
"Blood" for all creation.
Love prayed all night in the garden to
change the sin-sick sitch condition.
Love brought the blood covenant back to
the FATHER by going to the rugged,
painful cross.
Love knowingly knew He would be
beaten unmercifully for all who were lost.
Love had thorns placed in His head,
He paid that unpayable, irreplaceable,
significant, dreadful charge price.
Love went to defeat hell's kingdom,
dust beneath and came back with keys for
all who would believe.
Love knows we have the autonomy
to be His bride on the
GLORIOUS TRIUMPHANT DAY.
Love is accepting The REDEEMER,
The MIGHTY ONE, THEE CHRIST
because He loved you in AWEEE
of you...Love is.

122.

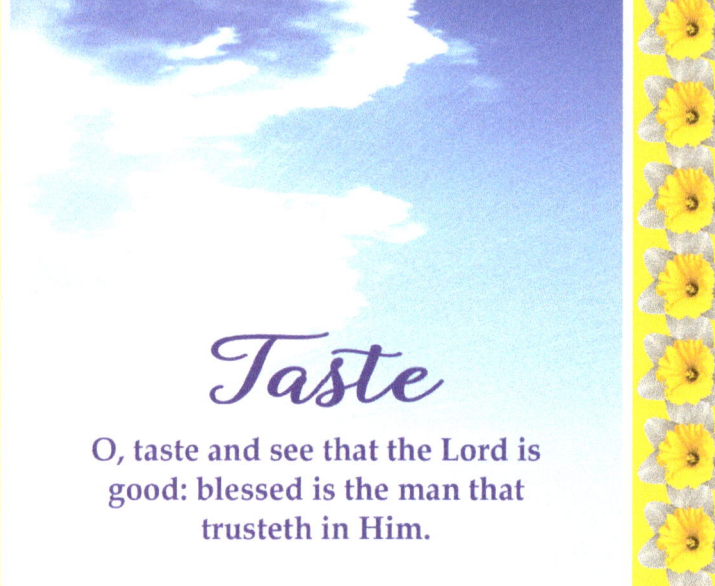

Tea Lady's Poetry of Love

# *Taste*

O, taste and see that the Lord is
good: blessed is the man that
trusteth in Him.

**Psalm 34:8 KJV**

123.

# Tea Chapter 9

## She's a Bad Mamma Jamma

## In the Kitchen

# Salt

Let your speech be always with
grace, seasoned with salt, that ye may
know how ye ought to answer
every man.

**Colossians 4:6 KJV**

# Kitchen Mama

Sitting in her chair at a table of manners, a
Superb Cook she is, seasoned with grace
and a teabit of salt. Mama says to Poppa,
"I'm about to watch my favorite show.
Join me in the kitchen and have a seat."
Because ebullience, laughter, and love are
Mama's signature acquiescing recipe to
follow and model after, while she's
preparing to stir by letting no ingredients
go to waste with each utensil in place.
Mama's Special Turkey Stew that she tastes
in three tea scoops is now on her countertop
for a slurp-up eat-all. Her pinches are
Teatop Excellent in Rosemary leaves for
wisdom.
Her Cayenne Chili Italian-style potent
pepper with oregano is for forgiveness.
She uses chives and parsley to festoon and
garnish her plates to show you how to
glitzy up for your date brunch.
She's optimistic about paprika-ing your
problems with celery sticks to be sautéed
for your taste. As she wears eloquence in
her apron while she's mixing and preparing
a meal fit for her bottle oil bran vase tea
maker — Kitchen Mama, who can cook from
any ingredients called herbal, tender, and
lean.

126.

# *Pray*

While the earth remains, seedtime
and harvest, cold and heat, summer
and winter, day and night,
shall not cease."

**Genesis 8:22 ESV**

Tea Lady's Poetry of Love

# MY PRAYER...

FATHER GOD
is that there
will be seeds always
to be planted in
fields for meals
for our children in
harvesting seasons.

128.

# Pray

Yet the Lord will command his
lovingkindness in the day time, and in
the night his song shall be with me,
and my prayer unto the God
of my life.

**Psalm 42:8 KJV**

# I AM PRAYER

I give hope for tomorrow when you call on
my name.
I am Prayer

I'm not discriminatory, racist, separatist,
or unjust.
I am Prayer

I'm kindled, inflamed like a torch with
fasting, and sealed by the
SPIRIT of PROPHECY and ADOPTION.
I am Prayer

I sit in the presence of my Father, asking
Him for you to be forgiven.
I am Jesus PRAYER

I am an open invitation.
Salvation is mine to give, my Lady Love.
Embrace your eternal life,
filled with love, peace, joy
in my stead.
I AM JESUS

# Take

And he will take your daughters to be confectionaries, and to be cooks, and to be bakers.

**1 Samuel 8:13 KJV**

# Cooking in Love

Momma's kitchen is warm with love.
It flows into her dining room and touches
every heart with each bite of her favorite
cuisines, healthy soups.
They're rich in flavors. It's something
mystically stupendous about how she
prepares her meals.
When you eat it, you feel you're at home.
The taste is magnificent.
It reminisces so many good family
thanksgiving gathering times.
None can compare to her hearty, savory,
robust, mouthwatering meals.
Momma's food has one-of-a-kind
flavorable seasonings in every season.
It sticks to your heart to let you know you
are loved.
Her soups herald, divulge in her kitchen
the spirit of joy, companionship, and
festivity.
It soothes and relaxes the atmosphere that
can relate to how GOD made everything
for our taste buds liking. In Genesis 1:29,
He tells us he has given every herb bearing
seed measurements, which is upon the face
of all the earth, and trees.
It is pleasantly blissfully arrayed
for his Tea Love.

Tea Lady's Poetry of Love

# *Loving*

Cause me to hear your loving
kindness in the morning,
for in you do I trust; cause me to know
the ways in which I should walk, for I
lift up my soul to thee.

**Psalm 143:8 NKJV**

Tea Lady's Poetry of Love

# Tea Chapter 10
## Walking with The King

Tea Lady's Poetry of Love

# Faithful

Your love, God, is my song, and I'll sing it!
I'm forever telling everyone how faithful you are.

**Psalm 89:1 NIV**

Tea Lady's Poetry of Love

# I am not Alone

I am not alone. I feel so close to you.
I am not alone.
I smell you amidst every aroma of
lavender, velvety honey milk, so creamy.
I am not alone.
I taste your goodness on my lips.
I am not alone.
I hear you whispering in my earlobe.
I am not alone.
I sense your presence over me.
I am not alone.
I heard your voice calling when I slept.
I am not alone.
As I breathe, I catch each breath you give
me.
I am not alone.
When I awake, you are right there with me.
I am not alone.
You will never leave me nor forsake me.
I am not alone.
Though I may be weary.
I am not alone.
You are my shepherd
JEHOVAH ELOHAY.
I am not alone.

136.

# Free

Now the lord is the Spirit, and where the Spirit of the Lord is, there is freedom.

**2 Corinthians 3:17 NIV**

# Walk On My Sister, Walk On

Walking with GOD so free and without
vanquish. He carries me during
vigorous times and with a pleasant
demeanor, which no one can see.
He revealed His presence so distinctively to
me. I see Him in my dimness, my misery, my
displeasure until I know them no more; their
presence can stay no more resting on
my pillow sheets.
In my state of confusion, He speaks to me
about a narrow roadway of escape.
His hand I had to hold while walking with
Him, His Voice, His footsteps keeping my
mind gauge in pace with His will.
He gives me power over the enemy
to put him under my feet. My life now has
been victorious, overcoming difficulties and
hardships. WHILE walking with GOD, there
are no more victimized mentalities of
challenges sitting on my fluttering cerebrum.
Nor open rooms available to intimidate,
attack, demoralize my place of leadership. But
it takes three to walk this journey; FATHER
GOD, THE SON, and HOLY SPIRIT, who has
no fault in the matter. Their batteries are
charged to full-service capacity. I need all
three to continue to jump-start me.
I'm Walking…

# Rely

Dear Sister-Friend, let us love one
another, for love comes from God.
Everyone who loves has been born
of God and knows God.

**1 John 4:7 NIV**

And so we know and rely on the
love God has for us.
God is love. Whoever lives in love
lives in God, and God in them.

**1 John 4:16 NIV**

# True Love

True Love is authentic, bona fide, and can be
truthful, indeed, in many associations that
are knitted together.
True Love is unchained, unconfined.
It cost nothing to share
but a willingness to bare.
True Love is friendly to all who embrace it.
True Love is sweetly endearing as the
countenance displays awe.
True Love is not mean, rude, or pretentious
towards anything.
True Love is reputable, warmhearted when
it lends a beaming brightness to another
that's in need.
True Love is heart-felt, lifting.
True Love is embracing the rocky parts of
your day.
True Love is sweet but not sweetened
enough to kill.
True Love is a sudden swirl of fun balls
when the excitement in your heart is so
overwhelming that it makes you feel like
you're going to burst.
True Love is exuberant from the heart-
throbbing beats that vibrate exhilaration for
the chest cavity in an expression of affection.
True Love is available to all.
True Love is beautiful, and beautiful is
who GOD made you and what
GOD birthed to all.

# Radiant

Your love, Lord, reaches to the
heavens, your faithfulness to the
skies.
Show me the wonders of your great
love, you who save by your right
hand those who take refuge in you
from their foes.

**Psalm 36:5, 17:7 NIV**

# Love in Colors

Love knows no black and white;
it's authentic in its peculiarity.
Love has no particular nationality of color
in a cottage house or a gorgeous
château on a hill.
Love is genuine, a witness, asserted like a
beauteous, aesthetic, stargaze dream...
Love is ineffable as a sun
shiny day theme.
Love is a radiate gleam, a glimmer
of the moonlight gate sparkling flicker.
Love is a charm
hung around your neck.
Love is an experience certifiable
with challenging urging demands in life
itself.
Love is incomparable, benign,
delicate, too...
It can be a bountiful delegation of wealth,
also a flower in full bloom.
Love is an undeniable energy brio
that attracts me to you.

# Sound

Blessed is the people that know the
joyful sound: they shall walk, O Lord,
in the light of thy countenance.

**Psalm 89:15 KJV**

# Blessed is a Teava Lady
## From Up Above...

Blessed is a Teava Lady from up above
who paces, strolls, and marches in time in
this universe.
She has been given life to obtain
acceptance and access to call on the name
of the LORD, who has died to pardon her
iniquities, misdeeds, and trespasses,
giving her a new birth with an original
ballad tune song...

Blessed is a Teava Lady who
Loves the LORD,
She dedicates orisons to heaven
She gives thanks to
I AM
THE CAPTAIN OF SALVATION
and comes to the altar face to face with
the covering angels from above...

Blessed is a Teava Lady who
has all of her limbs
that can hear the tea wind's sounds,
making mirthful, convivial, merry
conversations with her tea sisters around
the Tea Talk Tea Table...
BE BLESSED FROM UP ABOVE
TEAVAS!

# Seek

One thing have I desired of the Lord,
that will I seek after,
that I may dwell in the house of the
Lord all the days of my life to behold
the beauty of the Lord,
and to inquire in his temple.

**Psalm 27:4 KJV**

Tea Lady's Poetry of Love

# Tea Chapter 11
# Watch for Love

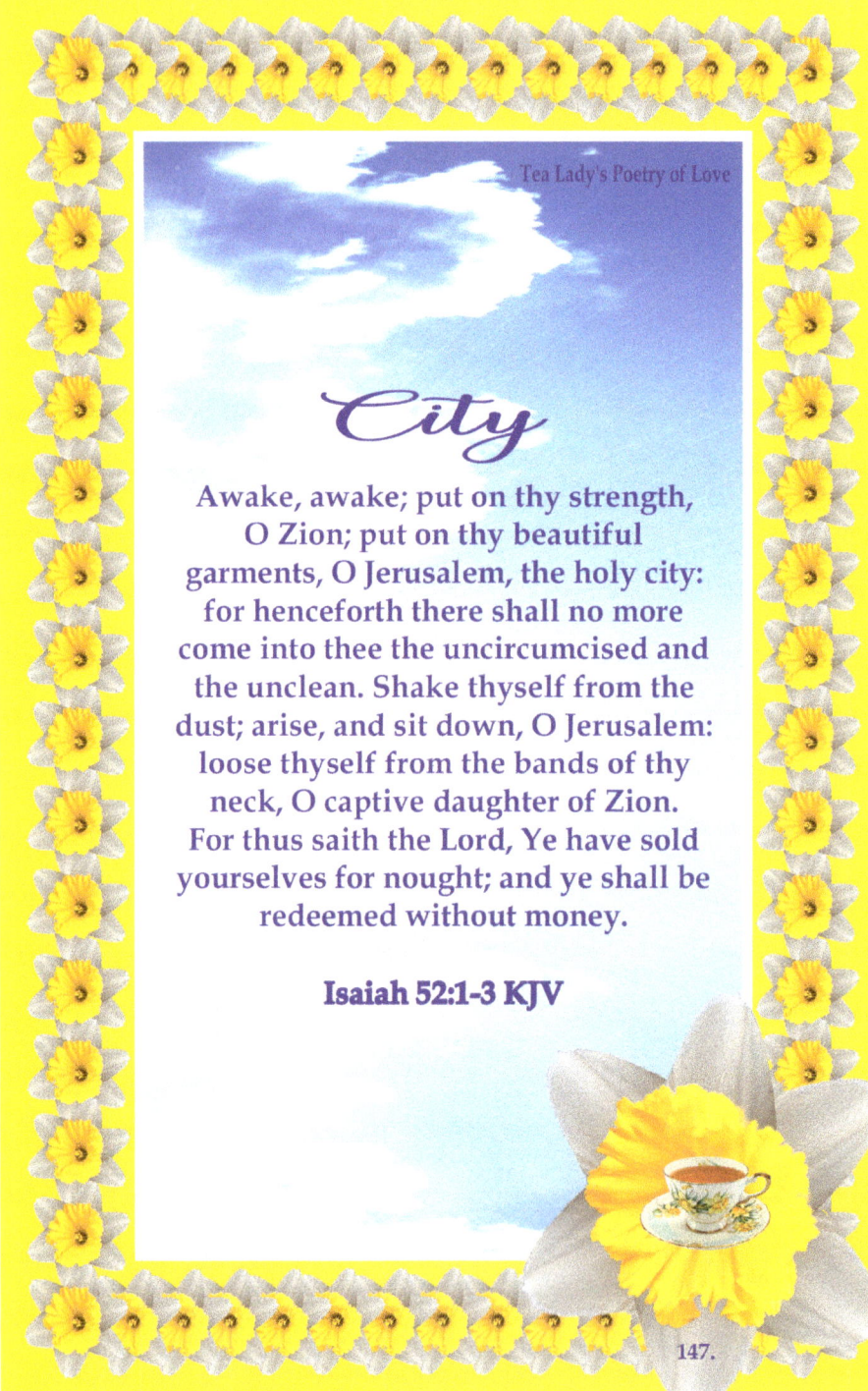

# City

Awake, awake; put on thy strength,
O Zion; put on thy beautiful
garments, O Jerusalem, the holy city:
for henceforth there shall no more
come into thee the uncircumcised and
the unclean. Shake thyself from the
dust; arise, and sit down, O Jerusalem:
loose thyself from the bands of thy
neck, O captive daughter of Zion.
For thus saith the Lord, Ye have sold
yourselves for nought; and ye shall be
redeemed without money.

**Isaiah 52:1-3 KJV**

147.

# Wake Up!

Wake up, listen to me.
Everybody needs to hear this; women, men,
boys, and girls. There is a war raging here in
society as we know it.
Families are being torn apart; inappropriate
relationships have bequeathed their part.
We must take action and get involved.
To save our children before they dissolve.
As we proceed in candlelight vigils for the
deceased, our communities prayers coming
together can endow harmony.
We must take a step in the right direction.
But without CHRIST, a cloud will cover our
perception. False prophets are on the rise,
killing their followers with no compromise.
Decisions are being made for you and me
without any agreement masking the truth
while people still need help
with the fewest signs of relief.
If we join forces collectively and step up to
the plate together, change will increase
positively.
JESUS is coming soon…If you have no trust
in him and don't believe, you won't achieve,
entering into
His HOLY ZION JERUSALEM SANCTUARY
for all human beings.

Tea Lady's Poetry of Love

# Pray

Ah, Sovereign LORD, you have made the heavens and the earth by your great power and outstretched arm.
Nothing is too hard for you.

**Jeremiah 32:17 NIV**

Tea Lady's Poetry of Love

# MY PRAYER...

FATHER GOD

is that your love

will be our guide

from your Heavenly

Divine Decree.

150.

# Heritance

Thy testimonies have I taken as an
heritage for ever: for they are the
rejoicing of my heart.

**Psalm 119:111 KJV**

## Let's Celebrate
## Our Tea Inheritance

Let's Celebrate our wins and losses that have
given us a voice to what we will pursue.
Let's Celebrate together like families do.
Let's Celebrate our Legacy History Heroes of
cultures who overcame, persevered in
CHRIST by keeping their dreams alive,
singing old gospel hymn songs to survive, as
we hold our heads up believing
JEHOVAH CHELEQ will continue to make
everything work out for our liberty and
freedom.
Let's Celebrate in the YEAR OF OUR LORD
two thousand and twenty of
His restoration. To uplift those who need
our assistance, our vote, our blood donations
to make it through struggles,
social injustices, neighborhood poverty,
catastrophic natural disasters, and this
unconceivable worldwide pandemic.
Let's Celebrate according to GOD'S WORD
with prayers for our lawmakers and
inner-city reformers.
It will make a difference in the nation's
capital for all who have endured.
Let's Celebrate our inheritance
Sipping On Tea Lady's
Heritage Celebration Tea Blends!

152.

# Mighty

The thief cometh not, but for
to steal, and to kill, and to destroy:
I am come that they might have
life, and that they might have it more
abundantly.

**John 10:10 KJV**

# Lay Down Your Shame

The enemy is cunning and manipulative.
He uses deceived works to ease his pain.
Spinning in a cycle of, "What should I do?"
Ladies, lay down your shame; it's the right
strategy to do... It's a game. The devil plays
over and over again about loving too many
and never loving yourself enough.
Let this not be your wrong path choosing,
my sister, or give in to his evil words and
selfish lies.
It's a game, Ladies. But, I tell you, he's to
blame for other's pain.
Put your faith in EL ECHAD; it won't stay
the same. Think of all of the lives that are
gone from this world. They didn't expect a
premature expiration date.
The Bible says that "the devil comes like a
thief in the night," so you have to be
equipped, inculcated with astute advice.
Don't let the enemy play mind games with
you and make you think that you have all of
the time in the world to be rescued.
Turn your life over to JESUS.
Why wait? Do it now!
It's your goal of hearts for
eternal life.

154.

# Choose

Butter and honey shall they eat, that they may know to refuse the evil, and choose the good.

**Isaiah 7:15 KJV**

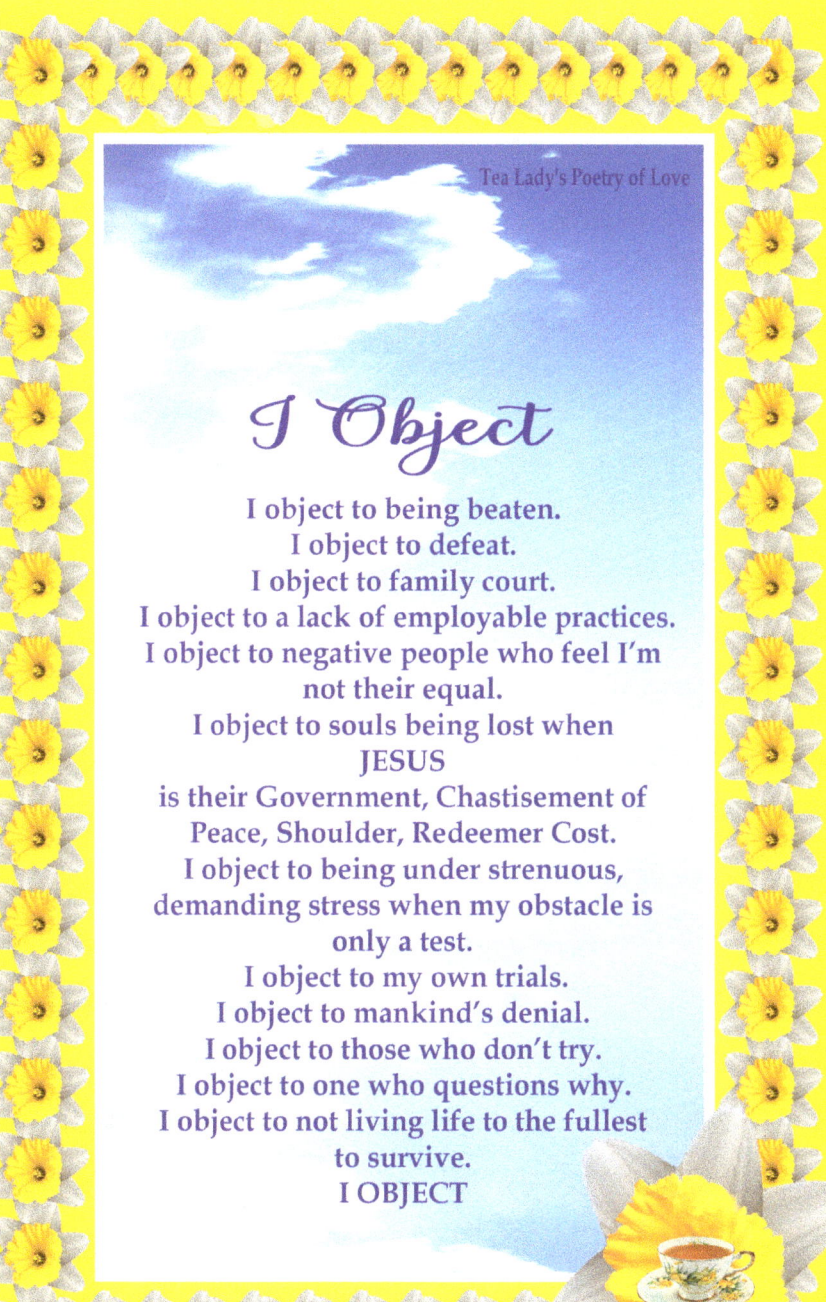

# I Object

I object to being beaten.
I object to defeat.
I object to family court.
I object to a lack of employable practices.
I object to negative people who feel I'm
not their equal.
I object to souls being lost when
JESUS
is their Government, Chastisement of
Peace, Shoulder, Redeemer Cost.
I object to being under strenuous,
demanding stress when my obstacle is
only a test.
I object to my own trials.
I object to mankind's denial.
I object to those who don't try.
I object to one who questions why.
I object to not living life to the fullest
to survive.
I OBJECT

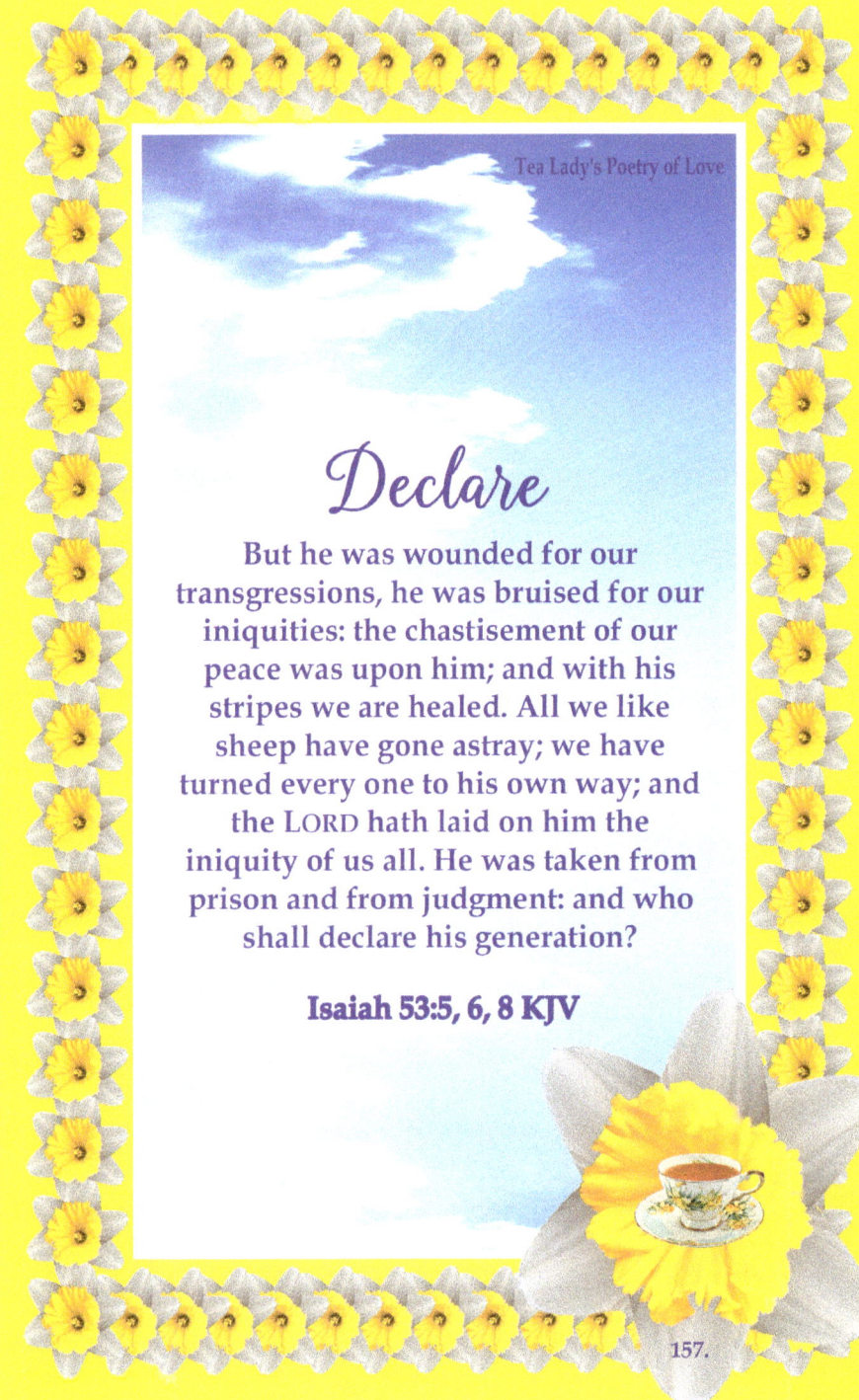

# Declare

But he was wounded for our transgressions, he was bruised for our iniquities: the chastisement of our peace was upon him; and with his stripes we are healed. All we like sheep have gone astray; we have turned every one to his own way; and the LORD hath laid on him the iniquity of us all. He was taken from prison and from judgment: and who shall declare his generation?

**Isaiah 53:5, 6, 8 KJV**

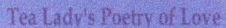
Tea Lady's Poetry of Love

# Take Off and Be Clothed By Love

Take off and be Clothed by Love
to declare to this generation that we are
not weak in the battle of defeat.
Take off and be Clothed by Love
to steadfastly position yourself with
The BREAD OF LIFE, The LOGOS,
The HOLY ONE,
who was cut off out of the land of the
living to die for the people's
AFFLICTIONS.
Take off and be Clothed by Love
He made his grave with the wicked, and
with His faultless, innocent, unsullied,
descent bloodline, there was no need for
repentance, neither any deceit found in
his mouth.
Take off and be Clothed by Love
Yet it pleased ALPHA AND OMEGA to
bruise JESUS for our sake.
Take off and be Clothed by Love
He was wounded for our transgressions
to bear our generation's shame.

158.

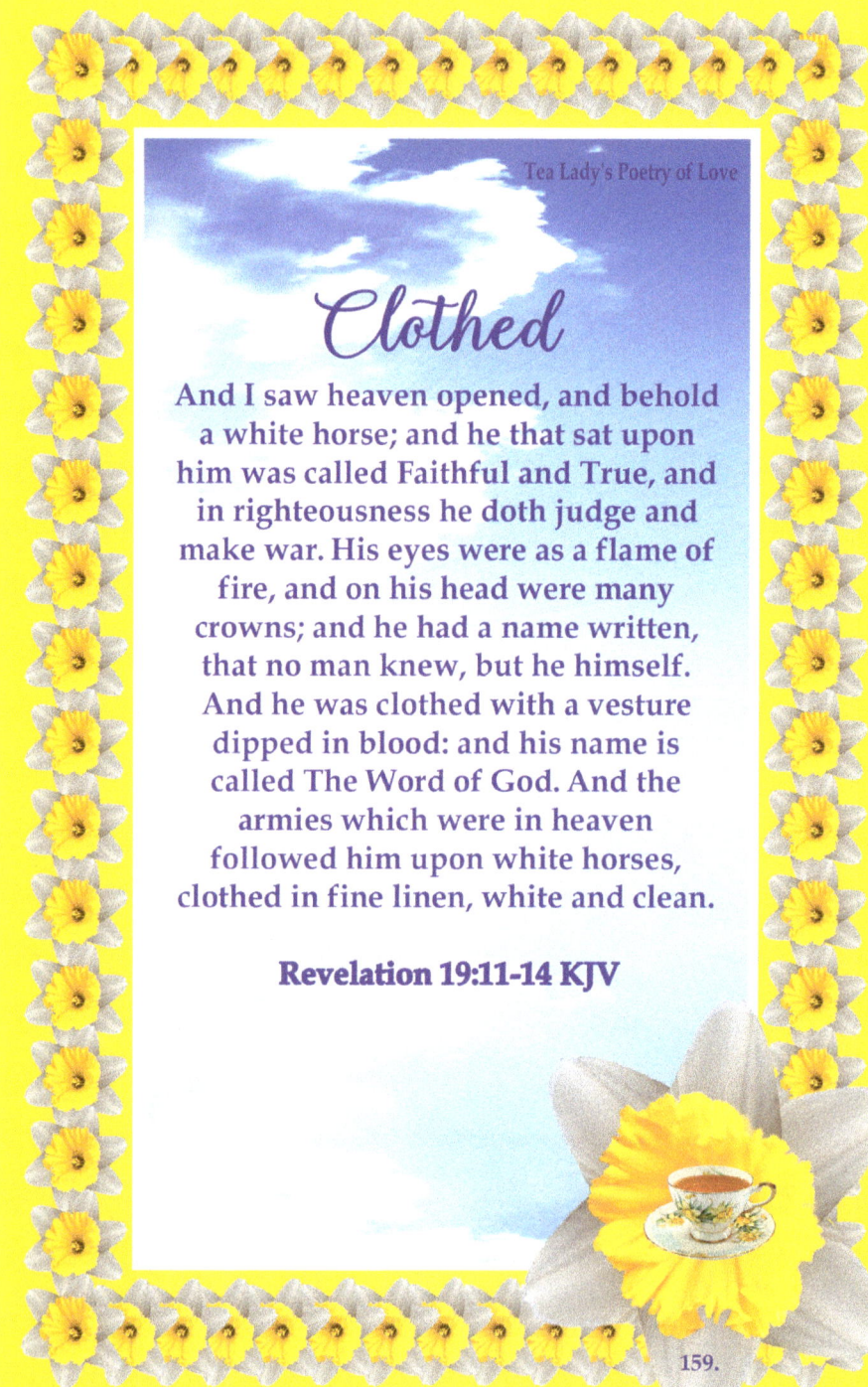

# Clothed

And I saw heaven opened, and behold a white horse; and he that sat upon him was called Faithful and True, and in righteousness he doth judge and make war. His eyes were as a flame of fire, and on his head were many crowns; and he had a name written, that no man knew, but he himself. And he was clothed with a vesture dipped in blood: and his name is called The Word of God. And the armies which were in heaven followed him upon white horses, clothed in fine linen, white and clean.

**Revelation 19:11-14 KJV**

# I'm on My Way

Seeing JEHOVAH LORD GOD's face
shining as a light saying, come on my
daughter into this very incredible sight.
I need you to get ready to receive my new
heavenly robe, pure, holy,
with the PANOPLY GRANDEUR OF GLORY,
draped in the way of the
PRINCE OF PEACE rectitude,
He bestowed.
His door swings spaciously open.
Don't hesitate anymore.
Look up! Look up!
JEHOVAH's ROSIE DAUGHTERS!
See Him coming on His white horse with
majesty. Ready to take us beyond His
Pearly Gates. As His WORD says, these
sayings are faithful and true: because
EL CHANNUN of the holy prophets sent
His angel to show unto his servants the
things which must shortly be done.
Angels are awaiting, come on, come on,
come back with me... He's awaiting our
arrival, so come on, come on.
He's your ROSE OF SHARON.
Come on back with me,
my Vanilla Fudge Rosie Love.

160.

# Prepare

In my Father's house are many mansions: if it were not so, I would have told you. I go to prepare a place for you. And if I go and prepare a place for you, I will come again, and receive you unto myself; that where I am, there ye may be also. And whither I go ye know, and the way ye know.

**John 14:2-4 KJV**

# A Better Place

GOD has a better place, Teavas; it never was his desired plan to leave us here on this terrene.
One day and it won't be long.
He ordained The PRINCE OF LIFE, The NAZARENE, to bring us home.
I'm on my way, but before I go.
I want to leave you with this love note message about His endless love all about you because it won't be a funfest unless you're at the CELEBRATION BALL for all. Celebrating with the angels, the elders, and saints to His eternal no end.
He's here in his GLORIFIED HEADQUARTERS CLOUDS, checking your name off on His scrolls to usher you into your new estate mansion, in this aging day, for believers now.
I can't wait to see my residing loved ones waiting at this wedding feast.
WOWEE, what an incredible sight it's going to be to see Mary and Joseph, Peter and John, Moses and Elijah welcoming us with felicity, blessedness, excitement, and blissfulness to the
LORD'S GREATEST HARVEST FEAST!

# Kiss

Let him kiss me with the kisses of his mouth: for thy love is better than wine.

**Song of Solomon 1:2 KJV**

# Blow a Kiss

Time and chance are something we do
not have liberal or bounteous time to
dissipate.
SO BLOW A KISS!
It's something very valuable.
Time and chance play vital roles if we are
attentive.
SO BLOW A KISS!
Like the coronavirus has taken many
lives of our dearest ones who didn't get a
chance to say goodbye to their loved ones
or write letters saying,
"Forever, you will always be forever
deeply loved; I Love you."
"You will forever have a pitter-patter
keynote throb in the sublime centerpiece
of my thoughts and essence forever."
It's real. You can be taken in a moment in
a twinkling of the eyes.
SO BLOW A KISS and say a prayer for
all those you adored, and this will let you
know JEHOVAH GOD is in control of
His throne and close by.
SO BLOW A KISS!

# *Voice*

Listen! The voice, the cry of the
daughters of my people from a far
country: Is not the Lord in Zion? Is
not her King in her?

**Jeremiah 8:19 NKJV**

# Tea Chapter 12
## The Lord
## Hears Your Cries

# Cry

Thou tellest my wanderings: put thou
my tears into thy bottle: are they not
in thy book?
When I cry unto thee, then shall mine
enemies turn back: this I know; for
God is for me.

**Psalm 56:8-9 KJV**

They that sow in tears Shall reap in Joy

**Psalm 126:5 KJV**

Tea Lady's Poetry of Love

# When My Tears Fall

The tears that suddenly fall
often speak to me when you don't call.
There are times in my life that are hard to
swallow painful thoughts.
The tears that I cry are not mine to own,
maintain, borrow, or retain.
So GOD, please catch each one of my
tears when they fall.
My puddles are like rain falls, dripping
and dripping that fill flower planter
with water sprouts.
I give thanks unto you, EMMANUEL, for
catching each drip-drop of my tears that
only you have counted that has
blossomed into divine stunning
Tulips and dazzling Daisies.
They're so tasteful, delightful in my
Daffodil Garden Bed Vineyard.
I'm so glad my aromas have spread into
a life of stabilizing, coruscating,
organizing
ROOT BUD FLOWERETTES.
When my tears fall

168.

# Moments

For his anger endureth but a
moment; in his favour is life:
weeping may endure for a night,
but joy cometh in the morning.

**Psalm 30:5 KJV**

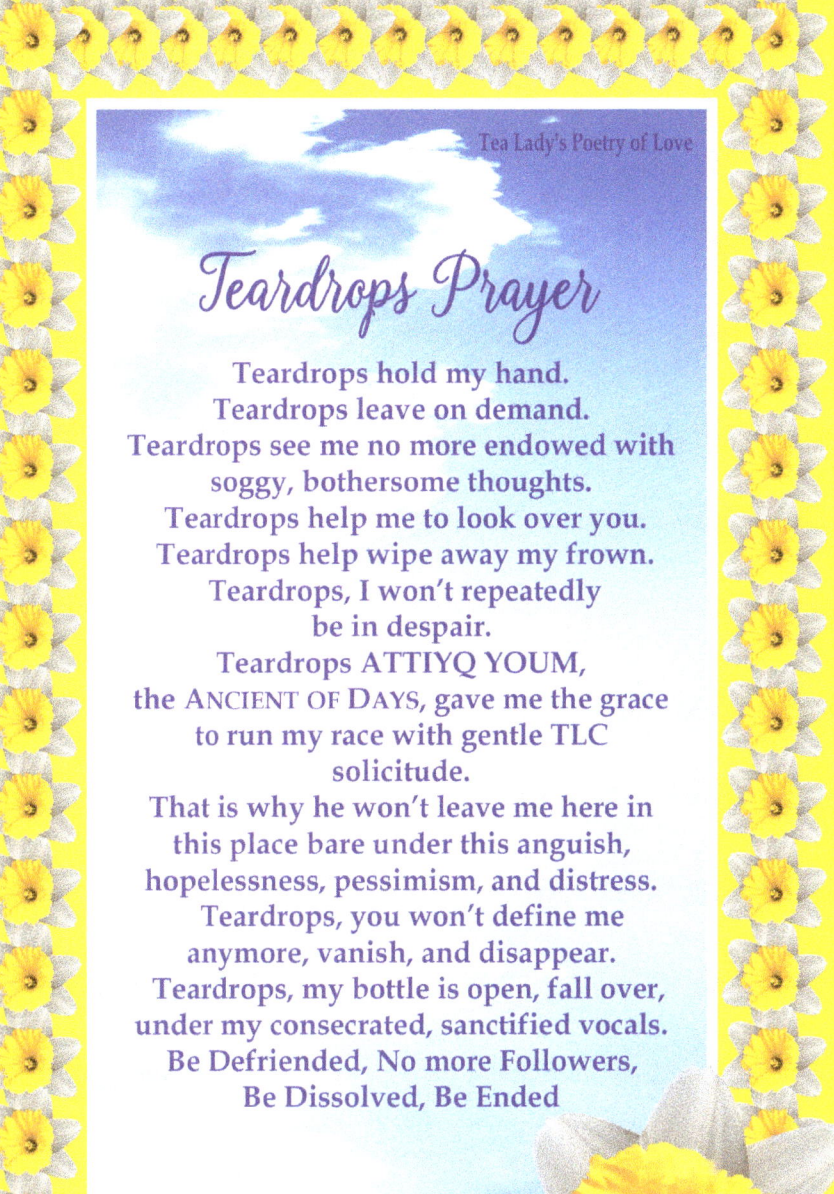

# Teardrops Prayer

Teardrops hold my hand.
Teardrops leave on demand.
Teardrops see me no more endowed with
soggy, bothersome thoughts.
Teardrops help me to look over you.
Teardrops help wipe away my frown.
Teardrops, I won't repeatedly
be in despair.
Teardrops ATTIYQ YOUM,
the ANCIENT OF DAYS, gave me the grace
to run my race with gentle TLC
solicitude.
That is why he won't leave me here in
this place bare under this anguish,
hopelessness, pessimism, and distress.
Teardrops, you won't define me
anymore, vanish, and disappear.
Teardrops, my bottle is open, fall over,
under my consecrated, sanctified vocals.
Be Defriended, No more Followers,
Be Dissolved, Be Ended

# *Yours*

And he said, Hearken ye, all Judah, and ye inhabitants of Jerusalem, and thou king Jehoshaphat, Thus saith the Lord unto you, Be not afraid nor dismayed by reason of this great multitude; for the battle *is* not yours, but God's.

**2 Chronicles 20:15 KJV**

# The Battle

This battle is not yours, my sister.
YAHWEH-SHALOM has sacrificed His
ETERNAL SON.
Give everything over to Him today;
those disappointments and perturbations
all belong to him.
So, my MIGHTY VIRTUOUS SISTER, you're
not in this battle alone.
CHRIST
has won it on your behalf.
His record is already recorded.
"IT IS FINISHED" IT IS DONE.
IT IS ALL GONE.
It's time to go onward, forward, across,
further ahead, with a new dance
and a new song.
To officiate in your position as a
GOD-FEARING WOMAN who knows how
to officialize in life episodes,
occurrences.
Be on Arise, my sister, and Rise up into
your AUTHORITY ROLE.

# Above

The heavens praise your
wonders, Lord, your faithfulness too,
in the assembly of the holy ones. For
who in the skies above can compare
with the Lord? Who is like
the Lord among the heavenly beings?
In the council of the holy ones God is
greatly feared; he is more awesome
than all who surround him.

**Psalm 89:5-7 NIV**

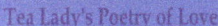

# GOD's Uniqueness

Most people look to Scientists for their
answers. But scientists all they can do is try to
describe the wonders of
GOD's Establishment.
It is by the words of His mouth that
GOD fashioned our world.
Everything around is made according to the
standard paradigm that He set before us.
So for each type of plant, animal, bird, fish,
and even people, our uniqueness
arises to shine.
The Bible says over and over that the just
shall live by Faith.
Faith is having no earthly limits to GOD's
spoken words over you.
It gives the competence to call forth those
things you desire them to become.
So my SISTER BELOVED, live in GOD's image
rather than allowing yourself to settle for
being a deflowered, blemished woman outlet.
Now go, my Authoritative Sisters,
SPEAK FAITH, WALK IN FAITH,
and
LIVE BY FAITH, in your uniqueness.

# Shall

And all things, whatsoever ye shall
ask in prayer, believe, and ye shall
receive them.

**Matthew 21:22 KJV**

Tea Lady's Poetry of Love

# Tea Chapter 13
# A Praying Woman

# Save

O God: incline thine ear unto me, and hear my speech. Shew thy marvelous lovingkindness, O thou that savest by thy right hand them which put their trust in thee from those that rise up against them. Keep me as the apple of thy eye, hide me under the shadow of thy wings.

**Psalm 17:6-8 KJV**

# Dial a Holla Prayer

JESUS is on the mainline; ask for what
you will agree with Him for.
Your emergency can be your children and
spouse dial Him at all times.
Your emergency can be your health;
dial Him. His WRI insurance demand
plan's coverage is unlimited.
Your emergency can be your finance;
dial Him to have your debt rates erased.
If your emergency is sickness and pain,
dial Him believing Him for wholeness
that gains healing that remains.
If you're in an emergency in the storms of
life when it rains, dial Him.
If your emergency is fulfillment with
contentment, smile when praying to
Him.
Whatever your prayer dialing needs are,
JESUS is there to answer you.
He won't hang up.
He will hang in there with you until your
need is timely manifested,
according to His will.

# Pray

My voice shalt thou hear in the
morning, O Lord; in the morning will
I direct my prayer unto thee, and will
look up.

**Psalm 5:3 KJV**

# I AM PRAYER

I pray daily; call me. I avail much when
done effectually and fervently by my
Righteousness.
I am prayer

I move by THE SPIRIT OF GOD
in every line and precept of my WORD,
call me.
I am prayer

The enemy is jealous of me and my
communion with my FATHER; YES
speak to me clearly and quickly.
I am prayer

I heal communities, rebuild, transform,
remodel cities, and nations;
call me.
I am Jesus PRAYER

I am treasurable in the wisdom of riches
more than you could ever purchase
in this lifetime, call me.
I AM JESUS

180.

# Pray

And all these blessings shall come on thee, and overtake thee, if thou shalt hearken unto the voice of the Lord thy God.

**Deuteronomy 28:2 KJV**

Tea Lady's Poetry of Love

# MY PRAYER...

FATHER
GOD
that your blessing
continue to follow
us all the days
of our lives in your
Providence.

182.

# Declaration

So they established a decree to
make proclamation throughout all
Israel, from Beersheba even to Dan,
that they should come to keep the
Passover unto the Lord God of
Israel at Jerusalem: For they had not
done it of a long time in such sort as
it was written.

**2 Chronicles 30:5 KJV**

# Prince D-Poem
## Grandmom's Story

I rejoiced for my soul's gladness when I heard
of your arrival from Daddy Dominique and
Mommy Felicia. Those words, "You're going
to be a Grandmom. It's a baby boy, my Poppy
eu," my nickname for you. It ignited in me a
love, lore, a love most incredible just for you
that will last a whole lifetime through. The
smile you had on your face. The first time I
saw you made me see GOD's aspirations and
future plans, He placed in you. You put a
hook in me to net my heart close to you,
"Poppy eu."

Prince, this poem is recited upon just for you.
A care, a care, a care. It's a joy, a joy, a joy
watching you crawl up and down the hall,
throwing your basketball from afar. Then, at
the age of one, how you quickly gravitated to
new words like star, dog, cat, and clap; put
Grandmom's heart into a pitter-pat.

It was exciting and messy to see you in your
Thomas choo choo train highchair wanting to
feed yourself while making a mess on the
floor, saying "Thank-you Mom Mom,
Can I have some more?"

Prince, to My First Grandson Born.
You are the most chivalrous, funnest little kid
who walked through Grandmom's Living
Room, and that's for sure!

184.

# Made

My words shall be of the uprightness of my heart: and my lips shall utter knowledge clearly. The spirit of God hath made me, and the breath of the Almighty hath given me life.

**Job 33:3-4 KJV**

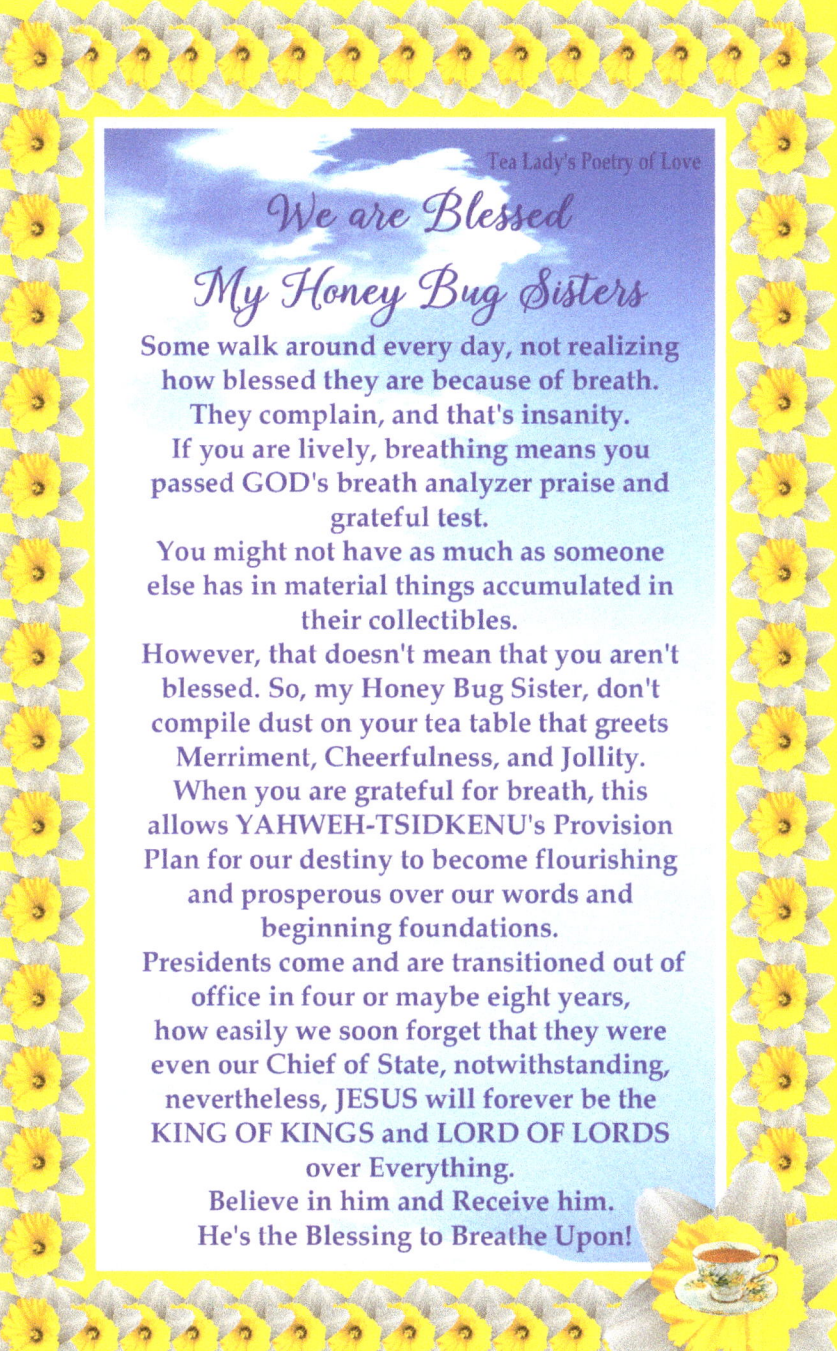

# We are Blessed

## My Honey Bug Sisters

Some walk around every day, not realizing
how blessed they are because of breath.
They complain, and that's insanity.
If you are lively, breathing means you
passed GOD's breath analyzer praise and
grateful test.
You might not have as much as someone
else has in material things accumulated in
their collectibles.
However, that doesn't mean that you aren't
blessed. So, my Honey Bug Sister, don't
compile dust on your tea table that greets
Merriment, Cheerfulness, and Jollity.
When you are grateful for breath, this
allows YAHWEH-TSIDKENU's Provision
Plan for our destiny to become flourishing
and prosperous over our words and
beginning foundations.
Presidents come and are transitioned out of
office in four or maybe eight years,
how easily we soon forget that they were
even our Chief of State, notwithstanding,
nevertheless, JESUS will forever be the
KING OF KINGS and LORD OF LORDS
over Everything.
Believe in him and Receive him.
He's the Blessing to Breathe Upon!

# Sleep

Ye are all the children of light, and the children of the day: we are not of the night, nor of darkness. Therefore let us not sleep, as do others; but let us watch and be sober. For they that sleep, sleep in the night; and they that be drunken are drunken in the night.

**1 Thessalonians 5:5–7 KJV**

# Sister Soldiers
## Wake up!

It is time now to wake up my
SISTER SOLDIERS!
The Church has been sleeping far too long.
GOD has called us to do a
superlative, eminent, and supreme work in
thee orb, principalities, global realm, for
others to live exceedingly with expectations to
subdue, conquer and become a Conqueror.
SISTER SOLDIERS! WAKE UP!
So many have been ASLEEP ASLEEP on His
Word that has been nourishing us too long.
SISTER SOLDIERS!
We're on the victory side for a Win, as the
SPIRIT OF TRUTH, CONSOLER, equips us
to crush and trounce.
SISTER SOLDIERS! WAKE UP!
The enemy wants people to lose their souls,
but GOD wants Women of Faith to play in
His leading roles.
SISTER SOLDIERS!
We are supposed to be soldiers on a
discerning purposeful post in His appointed
assignment. Therefore Sisters, be attentive,
on watchful duty, don't give the enemy your
dominion access roots that
GOD has Predestined and
Redeemed for You!

188.

# Pray

Remember the former things, those of long ago; I am God, and there is no other; I am God, and there is none like me. I make known the end from the beginning, from ancient times, what is still to come. I say, 'My purpose will stand, and I will do all that I please.'

**Isaiah 46:9-10 NIV**

# MY PRAYER...

Teavas, there's

no Omega with Yahweh

Until we meet for

Tea next time.

Tea Lady's Poetry of Love

To D. Pearce, Tea Lady Queen
Congratulations on your
Bestseller Book
from
Your Spiritual Daughters
God's Chosen Women of
Empowerment FM International

191.

## To a Treasurable Woman
## God has Anointed You

Oh, how GOD has anointed you to see the
people's needs, not just the saints under
the steeple.
All those who believe there's no hope, abused,
rejected, ashamed, or someone who subjected
their lives to reckless decisions.
Oh, how GOD has anointed you to hear the cries
of all the children left alone with no father,
mother, siblings, or gramps at home.
Their little footsteps do not know where to go,
running for love, running for affection, running
for acceptance, as you provided resilience,
stamina, endurance for them to ably run in their
growth stem race.
Oh, how God has anointed you to love all those
who believe they are unlovable when facing trials
indescribable. I know their distress touched your
heart; to write Poetry Tea Love Books that
inspires, reveals, encourages
Ladies with healing for their hearts, souls, and
thought patterns.
Oh, how GOD has anointed you to walk in the
divine calling He spoke to you. Yes, you heard His
voice, and we know it's true. Oh my, what a
first-class, first-rate, superb blessing GOD has for
you to continue showing His love and to reward
all He watches you do.
"TEA CHEERS OF SIPS"
TO TEA LADY, A TREASURABLE WOMAN
from
GOD'S CHOSEN WOMEN

192.

## Tea Lady's Tea Chapter

Tea Lady D. Pearce, a Certified Tea Specialist, is a native of Philadelphia. Her passion is God, who is the author and finisher of her faith. In 1997 she founded her nonprofit organization, Ladies of Legacy Dynasty Foundation, which provides clothing, shoes, and nutritional care packages to families in transitional homes. She also donates scholarship contributions towards college students' education and rebuilding, reconstruction of schools for orphanage children in Haiti.

In 2013, she birthed the Ladies of Legacy Tea Club, which hosts social tea events monthly that brew enjoyment, stimulating ladies femininity ladylike poise of essence in socialization. Tea Lady is a woman of strength, making a glaring momentous impact in our culture and society as she's empowering and building a Historical Legacy one Teava Lady at a time through Ethics, Economics, and Tea Etiquette. She's an author, poet, and writer of 15 Tea Books from her Tea Love Book Collection Series: Wisdom Jewels of Nuggets, Pearls of Wisdom in the Queen's Tea Cup, and Let's Have a Political Tea Party Ladies, to name a few. If you would like to support Tea Lady's Vision...contact us at ladiesoflegacysocietyteaclub@gmail.com